ALL ABOUT

SPECIAL CD INCLUDES OVER 90 TRACKS
FEATURING LOTS OF GREAT SONGS!

BASS

A FUN AND SIMPLE GUIDE TO PLAYING BASS

by Chad Johnson

ISBN-13: 978-1-4234-0817-8
ISBN-10: 1-4234-0817-9

HAL•LEONARD®
CORPORATION

7777 W. BLUEMOUND RD. P.O. BOX 13819 MILWAUKEE, WI 53213

Visit Hal Leonard Online at **www.halleonard.com**

ACKNOWLEDGMENTS

First and foremost, I'd like to thank my wife, Allison, for her tireless support and encouragement. I could not have written this book without you.

Special thanks also to Erik Schieffer for lending his bass talents and expertise to this project.

Kurt Plahna, my editor, has also been indispensable throughout this book. Thank you, Kurt.

I'd also like to thank Joel Dennis, who didn't realize what he was getting himself into, for mastering the audio.

And, finally, thanks to everyone at Hal Leonard for the tremendous work that you do.

This book is dedicated to my parents, Mike and Kay, and to my sister, Mika. The years of support from each of you means more than you know.

FUNNY STUFF

1) Q: How many bass players does it take to screw in a light bulb?
   A: None! The piano player does it with his left hand.

2) Did you hear about the bass player who locked his keys in the car? It took him an hour to get his drummer out.

3) A man gives his son an electric bass for his 15th birthday, along with a coupon for four bass lessons. When the son returns from his first lesson, the father asks, "So, what did you learn? "Well, I learned the first five notes on the E string." Next week, after the second lesson, the father again asks about the progress, and the son replies, "This time I learned the first five notes on the A string." One week later, the son comes home far later than expected, smelling of cigarettes and beer. So the father asks, "Hey, what happened in today's lesson?" "Dad, I'm sorry I couldn't make it to my lesson; I had a gig!"

4) Q: How do you confuse a bassist?
   A: Put one of his strings out of tune, but don't tell him which one!

5) Q: What's the definition of a bass player?
   A: Halfway between a drummer and a musician.

6) Q: What's the difference between a bass guitarist and God?
   A: God doesn't think he's a bass guitarist.

7) Q: How do you get a bass player to stop playing?
   A: Put a sheet of music in front of him.

8) Q: What do a vacuum cleaner and a bass guitar have in common?
   A: Both suck when you plug them in.

9) Q: How many bass players does it take to change a light bulb?
   A: None—they just steal somebody else's light.

10) Q: How can a bass player make a million dollars playing?
    A: Start with two million.

11) Q: What's the difference between a bass player and a large pizza?
    A: A large pizza can feed a family of four.

12) Q: What do you call a bass player without a girlfriend?
    A: Homeless.

13) Three men die in a plane crash and are waiting to enter heaven. St. Peter asks the first man, "What did you do on Earth?"
Man #1: I was a doctor.
St. Peter: Go right through those pearly gates.
St. Peter: And what did you do on Earth?
Man #2: I was a school teacher.
St. Peter: Go right through those pearly gates.
St. Peter: And what did you do on Earth?
Man #3: I was a bass player.
St. Peter: Go around the side, up the freight elevator, through the kitchen.

14) Q: What do you call a bass player with a beeper?
A: An optimist.

15) Q: What does a bass player say when he gets to his gig?
A: "Would you like fries with that?"

16) Q: What's the definition of a gentleman?
A: Someone who knows how to play the bass and doesn't.

17) Did you hear about the electric bass player who was so bad that even the lead singer noticed?

18) A missionary goes to the most remote part of the jungle. As soon as he arrives in the village he is to visit, he hears drums beating wildly in the distance. He asks the Chief what the drums mean. The Chief's reply is, "Drums play, good. Drums stop, bad." During the missionary's entire month-long stay he frequently asks the Chief about the continuous drumming. The Chief's reply is always the same. "Drums play, good. Drums stop, bad." Finally as the missionary is leaving, he asks the Chief again about the drumming. The Chief says, "Drums play, g..." "I know, I know," says the missionary. "Drums play, good. Drums stop, bad." "But why is it bad when the drums stop?" The Chief shakes his head and says, "Drums stop, bass solo."

BRIEF CONTENTS

FULL CONTENTS

Page   CD Track

INTRODUCTION

Welcome to *All About Bass*. Whether you're a beginner bassist looking to progress to the next level or you're still in the "bass players look cool" stage, you've come to the right place. Regardless of your reason or current skill level, one thing is certain: you know the bass is where it's at.

This instrument has it all. You want to make people shake what they've got? The bass guitar practically is funk. You feel the need to make the walls rattle? Rock bassists have been doing that for years. You want to play it cool? The bass can be the most understated of all instruments. And where would jazz be without that walking bassline?

There are many names for the rhythmic feel in music: the pulse, the beat, the groove, etc. While the whole rhythm section is responsible for making music move, the bass is perhaps the largest piece of the puzzle. No other instrument can get heads bobbing, fingers snapping, or booties shaking with such relative ease; and that, my friends, is power!

ABOUT THE BOOK

All About Bass takes you from ground zero and teaches you everything you need to know to become a serious bass player. Almost nothing is presumed with regard to your musical ability—we're starting from scratch here. We'll show you how to hold the bass, how to change a string, and how to get down with some serious grooves.

As the sections and chapters are somewhat self-contained, feel free to skip about the book. If you already know certain information, skip over it if you'd like, or read through it in case you need a quick refresher.

If you happened to buy this book before buying a bass guitar, you're in luck. Section 8 will help you pick out the bass that's right for you, as well as all the essential supplies that make you a true player.

Heads-up, Lefties!

This book was written from the perspective of a right-handed player. A right-handed player will use his/her right hand to pluck the strings and his/her left hand to play notes on the neck. If you happen to be a left-handed player, simply reverse these references throughout the book.

Here's How It Lays Out

The book is organized into ten major sections, which are further broken up into chapters. Here's a quick run-down of what to expect from each.

Section 1: Preparation: Before You Dive In

If you've never played a musical instrument, you'll need to start here. You'll learn about what makes up a bass guitar, what you're going to need to get started, some basic tips on practicing, and how to get your instrument in tune.

Section 2: Getting Started

In this section, you're going to start to learn about musical notation and the basics behind some key musical elements such as scales and chords. We'll also begin to examine a bassist's role in a band and start to play some simple lines.

Section 3: Getting a Feel for the Groove

Here, we talk about your place in the rhythm section and what that means. We'll look at various techniques that can add professional touches to your bass lines and continue our discussion on musical notation and basic music theory. You'll get to see what it's like to play melodies on the bass as well, and we'll talk about how to develop your musical ear.

Section 4: Styles

Section 4 is all about different musical styles. We'll dissect each one from a bassist's perspective, discovering what makes each one unique from the rest. We'll cover the various techniques and concepts idiomatic to each style and see how those are applied to real bass lines.

Section 5: Far-out Stuff

In this section, we'll take a look at various types of techniques and tricks for achieving unique sounds. We'll also cover some distinct basses not of the four-string variety.

Section 6: Jammin' With the Pros

Here, you get to study five full-length transcriptions of popular songs from bands such as Aerosmith, the Police, and more.

Section 7: The Gig

Make sure you read through this section before you book your first gig. It's packed with useful info, from how to be prepared to what to do in case of trouble.

Section 8: All About Gear

Musicians tend to develop a disease called G.A.S. (Gear Acquisition Syndrome). This section will explain what you'll be buying to satisfy your cravings.

Section 9: Care and Maintenance

If you want to take good care of your new pride and joy, read on! You'll learn everything you need to know to keep your bass shiny, healthy, and happy.

Section 10: Who's Who

In this section, we'll look at ten of the most influential bass players in history and what they've contributed to the bass world.

ABOUT THE CD

Follow the audio icons in the book (see next page for Icon Legend) to keep your spot on the CD. The track icons are placed to the left of each figure. With the exception of tracks 93–97, which are panned to match the original recordings, the audio is organized in the following manner: When drums appear on the track, the bass will be panned to the left side of the stereo spectrum and the drums will be panned to the right. This way, by adjusting the pan control on your stereo, you can either isolate the bass part for closer study or completely remove it from the mix when you're ready to take the groove into your own hands.

The intentions of this CD are to offer assistance as you go through this book and to help make you a better bass player. However, the CD should not be used as a substitute for learning to read music. Rather, the two should be used hand in hand.

Tracks 93–97:
Bass: Tom McGirr
Drums: Scott Schroedl
Guitar: Doug Boduch
Keyboards: Warren Wiegratz
Tracking, mixing, and mastering
by Jake Johnson

All other tracks:
Bass: Erik Schieffer
Drum Programming: Chad Johnson
Recorded at Famous Beagle Studios, McKinney, TX
Mastered at the Blue Door by Joel Dennis

ICON LEGEND

Included in every *All About* book are several icons to help you on your way. Keep an eye out for these.

AUDIO
This icon signals you to a track on the accompanying CD.

TRY THIS
Included with this icon are various bits of helpful advice about bass playing.

EXTRAS
This includes additional information on various topics that may be interesting and useful, but not necessarily essential.

DON'T FORGET
There's a lot of information in this book that may be difficult to remember. This refresher will help you stay the course.

DANGER!
Here, you'll learn how to avoid injury and keep your equipment from going on the fritz.

ORIGINS
Interesting little historical blurbs are included for fun and background information.

NUTS & BOLTS
Included with this last icon are tidbits on the fundamentals or building blocks of music.

Preparation: Before You Dive In

CHAPTER 1
STANDARD-ISSUE EQUIPMENT

What's Ahead:
- The bass and its parts
- Must-have equipment for any bassist
- Additional recommended items
- General guidelines on equipment use and care

In order to get started, you need the proper equipment. In this chapter we're going to take a look at nearly all the elements needed to call yourself a bass player. The first piece of equipment, which should be fairly obvious, is the bass guitar itself.

THE BASS DISSECTED

In order to communicate with others in a specific art or trade, you need to learn some "lingo." Being educated about your chosen trade goes a long way in helping you learn from other people and resources—not to mention helping you to avoid looking foolish at times! Music is no different; there are plenty of new terms for you to learn. Since this book deals primarily with the bass guitar, we'll start by learning the names of all of its parts. So grab your chart, sterilize your hands, and let's start dissecting.

Note: If you're one of those thorough and prepared types who actually purchased this book before obtaining a bass, never fear! Section 8 will help you choose the right equipment for your needs. Check it out, go get yourself a bass, and meet us back here.

I was kidding about the sterilization bit earlier—but only in part. Though you don't need to go so far as to sterilize, it is absolutely recommended that you thoroughly wash your hands before each playing session. This will substantially increase the life of your strings and help to keep dirt and oils off your bass's finish.

Let's take a look at what makes up the bass guitar. It's comprised of two main sections: the *neck* and the *body*.

The Neck

The neck is made from a variety of materials, though usually from some type of wood. Maple is the most common. From top to bottom, we have the following:

Headstock: The headstock appears at the end of the neck, immediately after the nut. It's where the tuners are attached.

Tuners: These devices serve two functions. First, they're responsible for securing the strings at the headstock. This is achieved by winding the strings through peg holes and twisting the tuning pegs (also known as "tuning heads"), thereby applying the tension needed to hold the string. The second function of the tuning pegs is fine-tuning the instrument so that it will sound "in tune," both with other instruments and relative to itself, as well.

Nut: The nut is the small piece at the headstock–neck joint that holds each string in place via a slotted groove. It can be made of graphite, brass, wood, plastic, or other materials.

Strings: The strings are the only part described here that are often replaced. (It's not uncommon for a new instrument to come without strings. If this happened to you, don't worry! Chapter 23 will show you how to put them on your bass.) The strings, once strung from the tuning pegs to the bridge, will vibrate as you pluck them and therefore produce sound.

The strings are numbered from 4 to 1 (on a four-string bass), with the fourth string being the lowest-pitched, thickest (or "heaviest") string, and the first being the highest-pitched, thinnest (or "lightest") string. For basses with more than four strings, the lowest string will always be the greatest number, and the highest string will always be 1.

Fingerboard: The top layer of the neck is called the fingerboard (or "fretboard"). This is where your fretting hand works its magic. Though it's sometimes made of the same wood as the neck, it's not uncommon for a different wood to be used here. Rosewood and ebony are common, as is maple.

Frets: The frets are the metal wires that lie across the fingerboard, perpendicular to the strings. These are responsible for manipulating the pitch of the notes on each string. By depressing the string, it is "stopped" against one of the frets, effectively shortening the string's length. The shorter the string's length, the faster it vibrates; the faster it vibrates, the higher the pitch. So, as you progress higher up the neck (towards the body, as the frets get thinner), the pitch goes up. In interval terms, each fret represents one *half step*. This is the distance of one key on the piano, black or white.

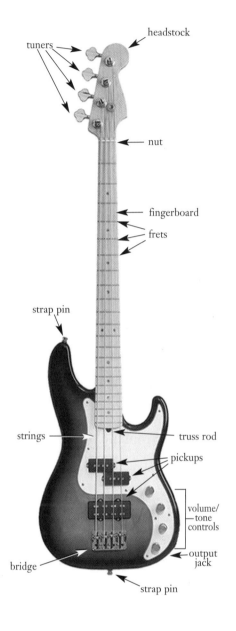

Truss rod: Running along the inside of the neck is the truss rod. This adjustable metal rod, which is usually accessed by an Allen wrench at the headstock or near the neck-body joint, controls the slight curvature of the neck. It's important to have this properly adjusted in order for the instrument to perform optimally (though it should already be adjusted properly on a new bass). This is part of what's known as "setting up" the instrument. Until you're completely acclimated with the bass, it should only be adjusted by a qualified repairman.

The Body

The body is the main chunk of wood that's responsible for creating the indentation in your ribs after years of playing. (That's what bass virtuoso Billy Sheehan says happened to him, anyway!) It's made from a variety of woods, with maple, once again, being a common choice.

Strap pins: These little guys are what you attach your strap to on the bass. The one on the bottom of the instrument (opposite the headstock) is also called the *end pin*.

Pickups: The pickups are responsible for turning the vibration of a string into an electric signal, which is then sent to the amplifier. This is accomplished by the use of magnets inside the pickup that create a magnetic field. When a string vibrates, it disturbs the field and creates the desired electric signal. These little devices are quite important, as it would be impossible to disturb the neighbors without them!

Volume/Tone controls: These knobs control the volume (loud or soft) and tone (bass versus treble) of your bass. Sometimes these are labeled with numbers: 0–10 or 1–10. If not, turning them fully clockwise is the maximum setting (loudest volume and brightest tone), while fully counter-clockwise is the minimum (no volume and darkest tone). Keep in mind that these can be independently adjusted—i.e., it's possible to have the volume set at "10" while the tone is set at "1," or "rolled off," or any possible combination in between.

Bridge: The bridge is responsible for securing the other end of the string to the body. Usually, the end of the string with the ball is attached here. Occasionally, special pickups, known as *piezo* pickups, are installed inside the bridge for further tonal variation.

Output jack: This is where you plug the cable into your bass. (The other end goes to an amplifier, pedal, etc.)

Because this action is so often referred to as "plugging in," this jack is sometimes erroneously referred to as an "input jack." However, the signal is clearly flowing out from the instrument to the *input* on an amplifier, so the proper name is clear. This is a good bit of trivia with which to stump your know-it-all friends!

Electronics: Housed within the body are the electronics. This is a somewhat daunting-looking (at first glance) amalgamation of wires, pots (short for "potentiometers"), other various capacitors, and the like. These all serve to create and manipulate the electronic signal. It's not uncommon for players to become adept enough to perform minor repairs or alterations on their own, though you should wait until you're more familiar with the instrument. Replacing pickups is one such common task.

If your bass has *active* electronics, a battery (or two) is needed to supply power. *Passive* electronics, which are generally more common, do not require batteries.

As mentioned above, the electronics in your bass should not be touched until you've become more familiar with the instrument. However, if or when you do decide to operate on your bass's vital organs, make sure it's not plugged into anything, for fear of an unpleasant shock!

PARTNERS IN CRIME: MEET THE REST OF THE GANG

If you possess nothing but the bass itself, you could technically be a "bass player." However, when have you ever wanted to—since high school, anyway—do the bare minimum? Your bass needs friends. It craves them. It longs for companionship. It gets lonely. Let's take a look at other essential equipment that no bass player should be without. Note that this list is hardly comprehensive; we'll take a much more detailed look at equipment in Section 8, All About Gear.

Strings

This may seem obvious, but as I mentioned earlier, it's not entirely uncommon for an instrument to come without strings. Some people pay music stores to string their instruments, but this is a very large waste of money in the long run. Stringing your bass is fairly simple and it's well worth

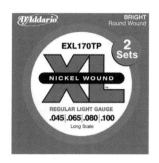

the time it takes to learn. Assuming you don't give up the bass as quickly as you did the skateboard (or one of your other fleeting fads), you're going to be changing strings many times throughout your musical career, and doing it yourself will save you a lot of money and many trips to the music store.

Strings come in different *gauges*, or thickness. The bigger the number, the thicker the string. These are often referred to in terms such as "light" gauge, "medium" gauge, "heavy" gauge, etc. Most basses have four strings (though five- and six-strings are occasionally used). Make sure you get a set of *bass* strings (not guitar strings!) that has the number you need. As I said, this is most often four.

Amplifier

Known by most as simply an "amp," the amplifier is the one responsible for getting you in trouble with your parents or neighbors. If you've never played a bass before, you might be surprised at how quiet it is when not plugged in; it's darn near inaudible. The amplifier takes care of that. The pickups on your bass send the signal out the output jack, through the cord (or "guitar cable"), and into the amplifier. There, the signal is greatly boosted to a level with which some actual damage can be done.

Amps come in one of two types: *combo amps* or a *head and cabinet*. A combo is essentially a head and cabinet combined in one package. Though they're more convenient in some aspects (they're usually lifted fairly easily with one hand by way of an attached leather strap), this is not always so. There are some instances when a head by itself (without the speaker cabinet) can be used, as well. For more on this, see Chapter 21.

Cable

It's not a glorious piece of equipment, but it is essential. The type you need is commonly referred to as a "guitar cable" or "instrument cable," and contains 1/4" tips on each end. Note that there is a difference between speaker cable and instrument cable, although they look very similar. Simply tell the salesman you need a guitar cable, and you'll be fine.

You can spend upwards of $50–$100 for the super-extra-awesome brand of cable, if you so desire. But when you're starting off, the $10 brand should do the job nicely.

Strap

If you want to stand up while you play, you'll need a strap. These come in all different colors and materials, so feel free to express yourself as you see fit. Learning to play standing up will take a bit of getting used to if you're accustomed to sitting, and you'll most likely need to experiment with the length of the strap so that the bass hangs at a comfortable level. This is often a compromise between the most practical and coolest-looking position—a decision with which every bassist or guitarist inevitably struggles.

Picks

Though most bassists prefer to play fingerstyle, there are times when the sound of a pick is desired. Many players, such as Paul McCartney, make regular use of both techniques. There are many types of picks, as you can probably imagine, but they're inexpensive, so experiment until you find the one that suits you best.

Tuner

A tuner, or *electronic tuner*, gives you an accurate measurement of the pitch to which your bass is tuned. These vary greatly in price, from cheaper designs that go for $10–$15, to expensive models that cost $150 or more. With a cheaper model, you'll most likely have to set a switch on the tuner for each individual string. Once you start getting into the $25 range and above, the tuners will most likely be *chromatic*. This means they'll respond to any pitch you play on your bass (fretted or open string) without you having to change a thing.

Metronome

This all-important (and too-often neglected) little device is integral to your progress as a competent musician. Extremely simple in design, its value is beyond measure. Basically, you set a tempo (see Chapter 4), and the metronome keeps a perfect beat for you. If you're used to practicing on your own with no other rhythmic device present, the first metronome experience will probably be a rude awakening. If you're just starting, don't put yourself through undue toil and agony this way; get one of these and use it from the beginning! I guarantee it will increase your worth as a bassist—especially to other musicians. There's nothing worse than playing with someone who's constantly speeding up and/or slowing down.

In the days before electronic metronomes, they used gravity and the basic laws of physics. To change tempos, a small weight was slid up and down a thin, vertical metal rod attached to a wooden base. When the rod was pulled out to one side and released, it continued to tick because of the gravitational pull on the weight. The farther up the rod the weight was positioned, the longer each cycle would take and, therefore, the slower the tempo.

Instrument Stand

If you have a case that came with your bass, a stand is not essential, but it's very practical. It seems that distractions often wait until you're seated and practicing before presenting themselves, and it's nice to have somewhere that you can quickly and *safely* store your bass during those times.

> Leaning the instrument against the wall is *not* a satisfactory alternative to using a stand. Take it from those of us who have experience in the matter. You can be sure, at some point, for some reason, the instrument will come crashing down to the floor and will likely have (at the very least) a battle scar to show for it. Don't put your instrument through this; buy a stand!

Music Stand

If you ever plan to make use of sheet music or instructional books, a music stand is a wise investment. (Balancing a book on your knee while trying to prevent the pages from turning is not an ideal practice condition.) A good music stand will allow you to adjust the height and angle of the music to your liking, allowing you to freely tap your foot (a recommended practice) without worrying about dumping a book off your lap.

GENERAL GUIDELINES FOR EQUIPMENT USE

There are a few things you need to know in order to keep your gear working properly. This will be covered in great detail later in the book, but a few things need to be mentioned here. Some of these may seem like common sense, but what's common to one may not be common to another.

- All connections (e.g., plugging the cable into your bass and amp) should be made while the amp is off.

- Get into the habit of washing your hands before each practice session. This will prolong the life of your strings.

- Wind up your cables neatly after use. Leaving them exposed on the ground puts them at risk of damage.

- Make sure your strap is tightly secured when standing up. For you and me, a fall from three feet is not particularly troublesome, but it could be fatal for your bass—especially if you're standing on concrete, tile, or some other hard surface.

- Spilled beverages onto your bass or amp could result in shorted circuits or other malfunctions. Keep them at a safe distance. No matter how convenient it may seem, your amp is *not* a drink holder.

- Start each extended practice session with a warm-up routine. See Chapter 2 for details.

There are plenty of other issues with which to concern yourself with regard to your equipment, but the above list is a good primer. Section 8, All About Gear, will address the topic, as well.

By now, you're probably ready to bust out some stellar grooves, and I admire your enthusiasm. However, there are still a few more things we need to discuss.

CHAPTER 2
LET'S GET PHYSICAL: STRETCHES, POSITION, AND POSTURE

What's Ahead:

- Stretching exercises to get loose and limber
- Attaching and adjusting the strap
- How to sit with the bass
- How to stand with the bass
- Right- and left-hand positions
- Clarification of frets and position
- Practice tips

You can hear the roar of the crowd from backstage, chanting your band's name in glorious unison. Your bandmates have finished their pre-show routines, and your stage manager gives you the signal. It's that time. You feel the adrenaline swell with your every step as you near the stage door. You're the first one through. At first you see nothing but the stage lights, but soon enough your eyes become acclimated and you begin to make out the legions of hungry fans that… *SLAP!* Wake up! You were daydreaming.

I'm sorry to be the one to burst your bubble, but you don't even know how to hold the dang thing yet, and you're already thinking about fans and stadiums and stage managers… OK, back to the task at hand. Let's try and stay focused, shall we?

STRETCHING

Before every practice session—and if you're a complete beginner you can consider this your very first—it's a good idea to stretch in order to help prevent fatigue and possibly injury. I know this may seem like torture at this point, but I'm going to have to ask you to put the bass down once again. This won't take long, I promise!

Playing bass, even while sitting, uses more muscles than you may think. Just as runners stretch before a run, bassists need to stretch before playing. With a few specific exercises, we can target the important areas and be ready to go in about five minutes.

Fingers

Obviously, the fingers get plenty of exercise when we get our groove on, so it only makes sense to get them ready for it. This exercise is quick, easy, and actually feels pretty good to boot.

1. Grab a finger with the thumb and first finger of the opposite hand.
2. Slowly bend the finger backward (away from your palm) until you feel a slight burn.
3. Hold for five to ten seconds.
4. Repeat for each finger and both thumbs.

Forearms

Your forearms (or your "Popeye" muscles) also get quite a workout while playing. This exercise gets them nice and loose, and there's no spinach involved!

Exercise 1

1. Extend your left arm straight in front you of with your palm facing out, as if making a "stop" gesture.
2. Grab your left-hand fingertips with your right hand and gently pull them towards you. You should feel a gentle burn in your left forearm and fingers.
3. Hold this for 15 to 20 seconds, then switch hands and repeat.

Exercise 2

1. Hold your left arm out again, but this time with your palm towards you, fingertips pointing towards the floor.
2. With your right hand, grab the back of your left hand (the side you can't see) and gently pull towards you. You should feel a gentle burn on the other side of your forearm.
3. Hold this for 15 to 20 seconds, then switch hands and repeat.

Arms, Back, and Chest

Exercise 1

This one will target your triceps and your back.

1. While clutching your hands together, reach straight up as high as you can.
2. Hold for 15 to 20 seconds.

Exercise 2

This last one will target you biceps, shoulders, and chest. You'll need to stand up for this one.

1. While clutching your hands behind your back, reach back as far as you can, attempting to create a right angle between your back and arms.
2. Hold for 15 to 20 seconds.

That's it. You've covered just about every muscle you'll use in your bass playing. Now, go find your bass and get back here on the double!

STRAP YOURSELF IN

Though you don't necessarily need a strap to play in a seated position (more on that later), most players leave a strap on their bass at all times. There are many different kinds of straps out there, but they all serve the same purpose. Some are easier to adjust than others, and some just plain look cooler. Regardless, hopefully you're going to be spending a lot of time under this strap, so make sure to get one that's fairly comfortable.

If your strap has a thick end and a thin end, attach the thick end to the strap pin near the neck-body joint. Attach the other end of the strap to the end pin, which is located at the very bottom of the body. Make sure the strap is well secured.

Drape the strap over your neck (like a camera), placing your right hand through it so that the strap falls in front of one shoulder and behind the other. You'll most likely need to do some adjusting at first to find a comfortable height. This may be easier to do while sitting down.

TO SIT OR STAND—THAT IS THE QUESTION

There are two basic positions that you'll need to learn while playing your bass: the seated position and the standing position. Since the majority of your time as a beginner will most likely be spent locked in your room honing your skills, it may seem as though standing with your instrument is not a top priority. However, if you ever plan to play on stage, it makes sense to start getting comfortable standing with it as soon as possible. There is a noticeable difference between the two positions, and the longer you go without trying to stand with your bass, the more pronounced that difference will seem.

With that in mind, we'll examine both positions here. I highly recommend you become adept at both early on in your development.

Seated Position

First off, you'll need a chair without armrests. They're nice for relaxation, but they do nothing but get in the way when you're trying to play. Ideally, your knees should be parallel to your hips, and you should be sitting up straight.

Most players support the bass on their right knee, as this centers the instrument nicely. The neck of the bass should be roughly parallel to the floor. This position will work with or without a strap, as the entire weight of the bass is supported by your right leg and balanced by your right forearm.

An important variation to the seated position involves the strap. For this position, a stool is recommended so that your knees will be below hip level. The idea here is that the strap will be bearing nearly all of the bass's weight. The neck of the bass will be angled upward (away from the floor), and the bottom of the bass will fall between your legs. If done correctly, this position should feel very similar to the standing position.

Standing Position

If you attempted the variation of the seated position above, in which you used the strap to support the bass, then the standing position is accomplished by simply standing up. When standing, the neck will be at an angle from the floor, which will make access to the lower frets on the neck more practical. It will also be more comfortable for your right arm.

The bass's exact position depends on your body style and will be slightly different for everyone; you'll simply need to experiment until you find what's best for you. The most important thing is to make sure you have easy access to the entire neck with your left hand and that your right hand and/or arm don't feel too cramped.

HANDS-ON EXPERIENCE: RIGHT- AND LEFT-HAND POSITIONING

The position of your hands and the way you use them is referred to as your *technique*. Taking the time to learn proper technique in the beginning will save you much trouble in the long run and facilitate your development on the instrument. The term for less-than-desirable technique is "sloppy." Don't be a Sloppy Joe. Pay attention now and save yourself from having to re-learn something later.

Improper technique can result in more than just sloppy bass playing. It can result in injury if you're not careful. It's not terribly uncommon for bassists and guitarists to suffer hand injuries at some point in their career—including many professionals. However, this risk can be greatly minimized by learning proper technique early on.

Right Hand

Your right hand is responsible for setting the strings in motion so that they'll vibrate and, therefore, produce a sound. This can be done in several ways, but for now we'll concentrate on the two simplest methods: *fingerstyle technique* and *pick technique*. (We'll cover more advanced techniques, such as the slap-and-pop technique, later in the book.)

Fingerstyle Technique

The most common right-hand technique is fingerstyle, so we'll start there. It's used in just about all styles of music, from jazz to hard rock, and is the preferred method of most professional bassists today. Here's how it looks.

While resting your thumb on the thumb rest or pickup, allow your first finger to come to rest on the high string (the thinnest string). The remaining fingers on your hand should be loose and slightly curved. Your elbow should be close to your body, and your wrist should be bent at about a 45-degree angle.

When striking a string, you want to push down on it slightly instead of pulling up or moving directly back across it. You should feel the string get slightly tenser as you push down on it. Once you feel this tension, gently move your finger backward, allowing the string to slide off. This will produce a solid, clear tone.

Pick Technique

Though the pick is somewhat frowned upon in certain bassist circles prone to snobbery, it's a legitimate technique that should be explored, if for no other reason than the unique tone it produces. The pick will produce a more cleanly defined attack, which may be exactly what's called for in

certain songs. Ideally, you should become proficient with both fingerstyle and pick techniques, as it can only broaden your palette of available tones and make you a more versatile bassist.

The pick, or *plectrum*, is a small, flat, triangular-shaped tool, usually made of plastic. You'll find that picks come in all varieties, so you may want to try out several before settling on one brand. Just as strings come in various gauges, so do picks. Since bass strings are much thicker (or "heavier") than guitar strings, bassists usually use heavier picks.

The pick is usually held between the thumb and index finger, with the thumb placed between the tip and first knuckle of the index finger. Some players prefer to make a fist with the rest of their right-hand fingers, while others fan them out from the first finger, anchoring one or more of them on the body of the bass below the strings.

Experiment with both methods to see what feels more natural. There is no "better" method, so if you're not partial to either method based on feel alone, just choose the one you think looks cooler!

To illustrate the difference in tone between the fingerstyle technique and pick technique, listen to **Track 1** on the CD. The first bass line is played fingerstyle. The second—played through the same bass, amp, and settings—utilizes a pick.

Left Hand

Your left hand is going to be getting quite a workout and performing slightly more demanding movements than your right, so proper technique is vital. A consistent, efficient left-hand technique will help reduce fatigue (and the risk of injury) and produce clean and clear bass lines.

The fingers of your left hand are numbered, with your index being 1 and your pinky being 4. Generally speaking, your left hand will be placed on the neck so as to match one finger with one fret. See the photos to the right for proper left-hand positioning, and keep the following in mind:

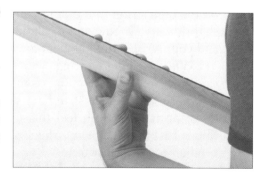

- Keep your left shoulder relaxed.
- Your fingers should be curved, as if you were holding a ball.
- Generally, you want to apply pressure on the strings with the tip of your fingers. There will be exceptions to this rule, but we'll address those later.

- Your thumb should be applying a slight counter-pressure about midway up the back of the neck.
- Keep your left elbow tucked in fairly close to your body.

Nothing to Fret About

As we learned earlier in Chapter 1, the frets are the metallic strips that are embedded across the front of the bass's neck (hence, *fretboard*). Frets are what allow us to change the pitch of each string. By pressing a string so that it makes contact with a fret, which, in essence, replaces the nut, the length of the vibrating string is shortened, thus raising the pitch. The further up the neck you climb, the higher the pitch sounds on that string.

> Most basses (and guitars) will have dots, or some other type of *inlays*, along the neck that make it easy to tell which fret you're at. Usually, these appear on frets 3, 5, 7, 9, 12, 15, 17, 19, and 21. Fret 12 is normally set apart by a double-dot (or a more elaborate inlay if your bass doesn't have dots).

When "fretting" a note (pushing down a string), you want to apply pressure just behind the fret itself—not in the middle of the fret area or directly over the fret itself. So, when you hear, "Play the note on the third fret," for instance, you would push down the string just behind the third metallic fretwire. It's this location (i.e., between the second and third frets, albeit closer to the third fret) that's implied when you hear the term "third fret." The term "fifth fret" would indicate the location between the fourth and fifth frets, albeit closer to the fifth. Notice the position of the fingers in the photos below.

> Remember, the strings of the bass are numbered 1–4, with string 1 being the thinnest, highest-pitched string.

So, if you were told to play the first fret of string 4 with your first finger, you would do this:

The fifth fret of string 3 played with your third finger would look like this:

The third fret of string 2 played with your second finger would look like this:

And the fourth fret of string 1 played with your fourth finger would be:

Assume the Position

As mentioned earlier, your left hand is generally placed on the fretboard in a one-finger-per-fret basis. So, if your first finger were placed on the fifth fret, for example, your fourth finger would be hovering around the eighth fret. The location of your first finger on the fretboard determines the *position*. When your first finger is at the fourth fret, you're in "fourth position." When your first finger is on the first fret, you're in "first position," and so on.

As you've probably noticed by now, the frets are wider in lower positions. Therefore, playing in first position will require a wider left-hand stretch than when playing in, say, tenth position. I know you're probably thinking, "But my fingers aren't long enough." Don't worry—everyone thinks this at the beginning. With practice, your reach will increase, and you'll eventually feel just as at home in first position as in tenth.

A WORD ON PRACTICING

It's been proven beyond a shadow of doubt that, when it comes to development on a musical instrument, slow and steady wins the race every time. This means that one hour of practice every day is going to yield better results than a seven-hour practice marathon on Saturday. This is especially true in the case of a beginner.

You're developing muscle memory when you play a musical instrument (especially a stringed instrument such as the bass), and the more consistent you are with your practice routine, the quicker this will occur. Think of a weightlifting program. You don't cram all your week's exercises into one super-workout on the weekend. You build your muscles slowly and steadily. So it is with practicing a musical instrument. Of course, if you have time to practice four or five hours (or more) a day, then all the better. The point is that seven hours on one day doesn't make up for an hour missed each other day of the week.

Here are a few things to keep in mind to assure that you're making the most of your practice time:

- **Start each practice with a 5- to 15-minute warm-up**: This warm-up period can consist of scales (see Chapter 6), arpeggios (see Chapter 7), or non-musical symmetrical left-hand finger patterns such as 1–2–3–4, 4–3–2–1, etc. The important part is to play slowly and cleanly during the warm-up. This will not only help to get the blood flowing, it will also help to enforce a clean playing technique, as well.

- **Use a metronome**: This is perhaps one of the most important things of all. Any time you're playing something in a specific rhythm, use a metronome. This will help you develop a solid sense of time and will also provide a way for you to track your progress.

- **Keep a practice log**: Write down things that you practice and organize your practice time based on what you need to work on. This helps you stay focused and avoid too much noodling.

- **Use a timer**: Set a timer for, say, an hour, and take a break when the time's up. If you have additional time to practice that day, do something else for at least ten minutes before you resume your practice session. This will also help you stay focused on the task at hand and keep your mind fresh and ready to tackle new material.

- **Transcribe bass lines from your favorite players**: Figure out your favorite bass lines by ear off the album. This skill may take some time to develop, but it's a worthwhile one for sure. In the beginning, start with simple bass lines that stick to just a few notes and/or repetitive rhythms; U2's "With or Without You" and the Supreme's "Baby Love" come to mind.

- **Listen to other instruments**: Listening to other instruments can help you avoid getting stuck in a rut (i.e., playing the same things over and over). The types of phrases you'll hear will most likely be new to you and can provide all kinds of inspiration for trying other things.

If you follow these guidelines, chances are you'll see steady progress and you'll never run out of things to practice.

CHAPTER 3

THE JOY OF TUNING

What's Ahead:
- Introducing the musical alphabet
- Learning the notes of the open strings
- Tuning the open strings

You can play all the phat grooves you want, but they won't mean a thing if you're out of tune. Learning to tune will take some practice, but if you're diligent, you'll be tuning in your sleep. Before we start twisting and turning tuning pegs, though, let's get a few other things straight.

THE ABC'S OF MUSIC: HOW NOTES GET THEIR NAME

Music is first and foremost and aural art; we enjoy music by hearing it. However, just as spoken language can also be expressed visually through written word, music, too, can be visually expressed in the form of musical notation. As language is built from the use of letters to form words, music is built upon notes that form chords or phrases. These notes have alphabetic names, just like our common alphabet.

In music, however, we don't use all 26 letters. We only use seven: A through G. After we reach G, we start back at A again. As we progress through the alphabet, the notes sound higher in pitch. This is most easily visualized with a piano keyboard.

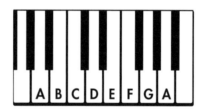

So, the C note that's labeled on the keyboard above is lower in pitch than the labeled E note, but higher in pitch than the labeled A note. What happens when we keep climbing in pitch to the next A note, or B note, or C note? Well, those notes are said to be an *octave* above. The notes have the same alphabetic name, but one sounds higher than the other. The distance between any two musical notes is measured as an *interval*. Different intervals have different names, and we'll learn those a bit later. Nevertheless, you've already learned your very first one: the octave. The figure below shows the octave relationship between several C notes.

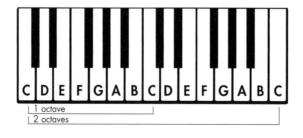

There's much more ground to cover in terms of notes and intervals, and we'll tackle that soon enough. But now let's talk about how this information translates to the tuning of your instrument.

THE OPEN STRINGS

Open strings? Meaning what? Open for business? Open to new ideas? No, no. In this case, "open" simply means unfretted—the pitch the string produces when you make no left-hand contact with the fretboard. The open strings are tuned to specific pitches, which facilitates the playing of scales and various phrases on the instrument. These pitches are as follows:

- Fourth string = E
- Third string = A
- Second string = D
- First string = G

Are you ready for your second interval? The bass is tuned in intervals of 4ths. This means that each string is a 4th above the string below it. Intervals have two parts: *quantity* and *quality*. We'll worry about quality a little later; however, quantity can help illuminate some things right now. We measure interval quantity by simply counting through the note names of the musical alphabet. For instance, from A to B is a 2nd. We know this by counting through the musical alphabet: A (1)–B (2). From A to C is a 3rd: A (1)–B (2)–C (3). How about from C to E? Just count up: C (1)–D (2)–E (3). It's a 3rd. See how it works?

A Synopsis on Soundwaves

Pitch is a common term that's equal to the scientific term *frequency*; the two are, for the most part, interchangeable. *Sound*, as you may know, travels in waves. The completion of one wave (from the midpoint of the highest point in the wave, down to the lowest point in the wave, and back to the midpoint) is referred to as a *cycle*. Frequency is measured in cycles-per-second units called *hertz* (Hz).

The closer together these waves are, the higher the frequency, or pitch. Therefore, bass notes have very long waves (e.g., 20 Hz)—in fact, several feet long if you get low enough—while treble notes have very short waves (e.g., 12,000 Hz). When dealing with thousands of hertz, we use kilohertz. So 12,000 Hz would be shown as 12 KHz.

Remember, the musical alphabet uses only A through G. After G, we start with A once again.

When we lay out the musical alphabet in one continuous line, we can see how the strings of the bass are situated in 4ths:

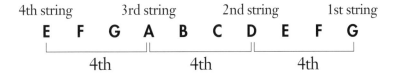

4th string		3rd string		2nd string		1st string
E	F	G	A	B	C	D	E	F	G
	4th			4th			4th		

- From E to A is a 4th: E (1)–F (2)–G (3)–A (4)
- From A to D is a 4th: A (1)–B (2)–C (3)–D (4)
- From D to G is a 4th: D (1)–E (2)–F (3)–G (4)

Incidentally, the strings of the bass guitar are pitched the same way as the four lowest strings of a guitar. The strings on the bass are one octave lower, but the notes are the same: E–A–D–G. This is why it's so common for someone to play both bass and guitar (such as Paul McCartney, Sting, etc.).

Now, let's find out how to make sure those 4ths are in tune.

GETTING IN TUNE

There are two main methods for tuning your bass. Perhaps the most common, for the beginner, is the use of an *electronic tuner*. The other method involves the use of a *reference pitch*. Here, we'll take a look at both methods, along with some advantages and disadvantages.

Electronic Tuner

There are many different types of electronic tuners, but they all serve the same purpose. Electronic tuners "hear" the pitch of a bass string for you and tell you whether it's sharp (too high in pitch) or flat (too low in pitch). You can spend $100 or more on one, but if you're just beginning, a nice $20 model should do the trick. If you buy a chromatic tuner, you won't have to make any adjustments to the tuner between strings. If your budget isn't incredibly tight, I highly recommend a chromatic tuner. They're not much more expensive, and they're well worth it.

They're all easy to use. You run a cable from your bass jack to the "input" (or possibly "instrument") jack of the tuner. If the tuner is not chromatic, then there will be some type of switch that you'll have to change for each string. This will either be labeled as "4th string" or "E string," etc.

Using a Non-chromatic Tuner

With a non-chromatic tuner, you may have to get a reference pitch (see "Using a Reference Pitch" below) before you can start tuning your bass; your tuner will only respond when your strings are close to the pitches to which they're supposed to be tuned. For instance, if your bass has new strings, and the tuning is way off, then the tuner will most likely not register. If you experience this, see "Using a Reference Pitch" and then meet us back here.

1. Plug the bass guitar into the tuner. Make sure the volume control on your bass is set to "10" (full).
2. Set the switch on the tuner to the string you wish to tune.
3. Pluck the open string on the bass. Make sure the other strings don't ring out at the same time. You can use your left-hand fingers to keep them quiet, if necessary.
4. Watch the gauge on the tuner. It will indicate whether the string's pitch is too low (flat) or too high (sharp).
5. Adjust the tuning peg for the appropriate string until the tuner indicates that the string is in tune.

Here are a few things to keep in mind when first learning to tune:

- Be patient; tuning is somewhat of a fine adjustment, and it will take some time to get it down.
- You will most likely have to pluck the same string several times while tuning it because the string will eventually stop vibrating and the note will "die." This is known as the *decay* of a note. This is perfectly normal and does not indicate a malfunction in your electronic tuner.
- Try to get in the habit of tuning *up* to a note rather than down to it. If you're already too sharp, bring the string down, past the in-tune mark, and then tune back up to it. The string will be more likely to hold its pitch this way.
- When your strings are in tune, listen closely to the way they sound together, two at a time. This will help to train your ear.

Using a Chromatic Tuner

As far as electronic tuners are concerned, the chromatic tuner is the way to go. You use it in the same manner as a non-chromatic tuner, but you don't need to worry about setting it to a specific string's pitch. The chromatic tuner will "hear" any pitch you throw at it. This means you don't need a reference pitch to use a chromatic tuner. You simply plug in your bass, play a string, and the tuner will tell you the pitch and whether you're sharp or flat.

To get your bass in tune, just play a string and adjust the tuning peg until the tuner tells you that you're on the right pitch (E, A, D, or G, depending on the string) and that you're in tune.

Tuning the Bass to Itself

This method of tuning is a bit more difficult than using an electronic tuner, but it's an absolutely essential part of your growth as a musician, because it helps to train your ear to recognize pitches and whether or not they're in tune. You see, with this method, you won't have a machine telling you what to do. You're on your own, and your ears will be the only judge as to whether or not your bass sounds right. Your bass entrusts its sonic well-being into your hands! Don't let it down!

Using a Reference Pitch

The first thing you'll need to do is find a reference pitch that's in tune. Here are a few devices from which you can obtain a reference pitch:

- **Tuning fork:** This is a small, inexpensive, metallic tool that's shaped sort of like a wishbone. You hold it by the single end and whack one of the two prongs against a hard surface, causing it to vibrate and produce a high, clear pitch. This is most often an A note.

- **Piano:** Since the tuning on a piano is relatively stable, it usually makes for an excellent pitch reference. Simply play the note on the piano that corresponds to the string you want to tune on your bass.

- **Guitar:** If you have a guitar lying around or are standing in the vicinity of a friendly guitarist, you can use it as a reference. Remember, the bottom four strings of a guitar are the same notes (only one octave higher) as the four strings on your bass.

- **Other instruments:** If you can't get your hands on the aforementioned options, there are other instruments that do the job, such as a harmonica and various brass instruments. Use your imagination! If you have an instrument that's known to be relatively in tune, it will at least get you close.

- **Other tone generators:** Certain electronic musical devices will provide tuning notes, as well. Oftentimes, an electronic metronome will be able to produce an A note, for example. Also, a pitch pipe is another common and inexpensive tone generator.

Tuning notes are provided for you on **Track 2** of the CD. You can match the pitches of your open bass strings (low to high) to the notes on the track.

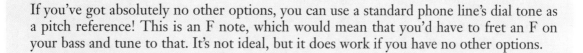

If you've got absolutely no other options, you can use a standard phone line's dial tone as a pitch reference! This is an F note, which would mean that you'd have to fret an F on your bass and tune to that. It's not ideal, but it does work if you have no other options.

The pitch you will be able to use as a reference will depend upon the source, but try to get a pitch that matches one of your open strings: E, A, D, or G. Obviously, if you have access to a piano or guitar, you could tune each string to match the corresponding pitch. However, since it's not likely that this will always be the case, it's essential for you to learn the following tuning method.

Relative Tuning

This is the most common tuning method and is usually the first that each player learns. (We'll cover other tuning methods in a moment.) It works on the principal that the bass is tuned in 4th intervals, but that's not terribly important at this time. All you need to remember is this simple formula: fifth fret = open string. That is to say, the note at the fifth fret of one string produces the same note as the next highest (in pitch) open string.

With this method, as long as you have one of your strings in tune by using a reference pitch, you can tune the other three strings to it. It's best to use an E as a reference pitch with this method. If you were able to do this, and, as a result, have your low E string in tune, then follow these steps to tune the rest of your bass's strings.

don't
forget

> If you use a reference pitch other than E, then you'll need to tune the remaining three strings to it. So that may mean you'll have to backtrack a little bit. For instance, if your reference pitch was A, you'd need to tune the fifth fret of the E string to the open A string, instead of vice versa.

1. Play the fifth fret of the low E string, making sure that your finger does not touch the A string. Pluck the low E string, then the open A string (so they ring together). These notes should be the same. If the A string is lower in pitch (flat), turn its tuning peg so that the pitch is raised. If the A string is higher in pitch (sharp), turn its tuning peg so that the pitch drops. (Since your left-hand finger is on the fifth fret, you'll need to use your right hand to reach over and turn the tuning peg.)

Once you get the pitches close, you'll begin to hear a wavering sound as the two strings ring together. This is referred to as *beats*. The faster the beats occur, the more the strings are out of tune. The slower the beats, the closer you are to being in tune. When the beats have completely stopped, the two strings are in tune.

Once you get the A string in tune, proceed to the next step.

2. Play the fifth fret of the A string, making sure that your finger does not touch the D string. Pluck the A string, then the open D string. Use the same process as above to get the open D string in tune with the fifth fret of the A string.

3. Play the fifth fret of the D string, making sure that your finger does not touch the G string. Pluck the D string, then the open G string. Use the same process as above to get the open G string in tune with the fifth fret of the D string.

That's it. Your bass should now be in tune.

Tuning With Harmonics

Another common tuning method involves *harmonics*. A harmonic is achieved by lightly touching the string over certain frets. The result is a chime-like note that's more pure-sounding than standard notes. You can play many harmonics along the string, but the most common can be found over the fifth, seventh, and twelfth frets.

To tune using harmonics, you need to remember this formula: fifth-fret harmonic equals seventh-fret harmonic. That is to say, the fifth-fret harmonic of one string produces the same note as the seventh-fret harmonic of the next highest (in pitch) string. Assuming your low E string is in tune, follow these steps to tune the rest of your bass with harmonics.

1. Place your first finger lightly on the E string (don't push the string down) directly above the fifth fretwire. Pluck the string and then immediately remove your left-hand finger. The

harmonic should continue to ring. Now use your third or fourth finger and touch the A string directly over the seventh fretwire. Pluck the string and immediately remove your left-hand finger. These two notes should match. Adjust the tuning peg of the A string to match the pitch of the E string. (You may need to repeat the process a few times.)

2. Now play the fifth-fret harmonic on the A string and then the seventh-fret harmonic on the D string. Adjust the tuning peg of the D string until its pitch matches that of the A string.

3. Finally, play the fifth-fret harmonic of the D string and then the seventh-fret harmonic on the G string. Adjust the tuning peg of the G string until its pitch matches that of the D string.

Listen to **Track 3** on the CD to hear examples of strings being tuned with harmonics. Notice how the beats steadily decrease until the strings are in tune.

Your bass should now be in tune.

There are other tuning methods that are commonly used, which you'll undoubtedly encounter as you progress throughout the years, but the methods given here should serve your purposes well for the duration of your musical career. The other variations are, more than anything, a matter of personal preference.

Getting Started

CHAPTER 4
MUSICAL NOTATION LINGO: THE BASICS

What's Ahead:
- Musical symbols on a staff
- Rhythms and division of measures
- Key-signature basics

Being able to read music is an important step to becoming an accomplished musician. Yes, there are many, many famous bass players (as well as guitarists and pianists) who never learned how to read music. Paul McCartney is one such famous example. It's true that reading music won't make you a better musician, per se, but it will allow you to communicate with other musicians with great ease, which will, in turn, increase your general musicianship. If there's an easy way and a hard way to do things, being an illiterate musician is definitely the hard way. It certainly can be done, but the process of learning to read music is so painless that there's really no excuse. Take some advice from Nike: Just do it!

MUSIC NOTATION SYMBOLS (WHAT ARE ALL THOSE DOTS, LINES, AND NUMBERS, ANYWAY?)

Let's take a look at what goes into music notation. Here, we'll take a quick look at some music and identify the key elements that you need to know.

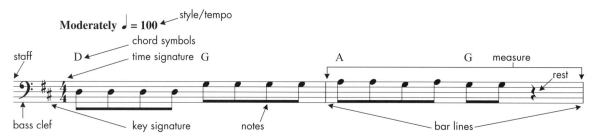

- **Staff**: The staff is the collection of lines on which music is written. Each line and each space between the lines represent different notes. The notes ascend in pitch from low to high. So a note on the bottom line of the staff sounds lower in pitch than a note on the top line.
- **Bass clef**: The bass clef is the first symbol you see on the staff when reading music for the bass. A clef tells the performer what notes the staff will represent. There are several different kinds of clefs, with bass clef and treble clef being the most common. With each different clef, the lines and spaces of the staff are assigned different notes. However, you'll only be reading bass clef, so you won't need to concern yourself with other clefs—unless you're one of those over-achiever types!
- **Key signature**: This is a collection of sharp (♯) or flat (♭) symbols at the beginning of the staff that tells the performer the song's *key*. We'll look more in depth at keys later. (No, it has nothing do with those jangly things you're always losing.)
- **Time signature**: These numbers indicate how the song is rhythmically structured. Both numbers have a specific purpose, which we'll soon discover.

- **Notes**: These are the little round things that are dotted all over the staff. They tell you which pitches to play and in what rhythm.
- **Rests**: A rest symbol doesn't mean you get to take a nap. It means to be quiet for a specific amount of time. You can think of it as a silent note.
- **Style/tempo**: This appears at the beginning of a musical piece and lets the performer know the music's style (rock, Latin, blues, etc.) and the speed of the beat.
- **Chord symbols**: In pop music, these are often used to indicate which chord is sounding at specific points in the music. Even though bassists rarely play chords (we play mostly single notes), it helps to know them when creating our bass lines.
- **Measure**: This is a unit of music between two bar lines. They're used to help keep your place in the music and are often numbered for quick reference (e.g., "Take it from measure 28!").
- **Bar lines**: These lines mark off each measure. They occur in regularity after a specific number of beats (which depends on the time signature).

The Notes on the Staff

As mentioned earlier, each line and space on the staff represents a musical pitch, or note. Since this is a bass book, and you (hopefully) are playing a bass, we'll concentrate on the bass clef. So, when you see this symbol (𝄢), you'll recognize the names of the notes on the lines and spaces of the staff.

From low to high, the lines of the staff are: G, B, D, F, A. The spaces are, from low to high: A, C, E, G.

G B D F A A C E G

To make these easier to memorize, people often assign words to each letter to make a phrase. For instance, "**G**ood **B**oys **D**o **F**ine **A**lways" is often used for the lines, while "**A**ll **C**ows **E**at **G**rass" works nicely for the spaces. (Many people come up with less-wholesome versions, but that's not appropriate material for this book!)

Notice that, when viewed together, the notes ascend straight up through the musical alphabet.

G A B C D E F G A

Ledger Lines

Since our instrument is capable of playing notes that are higher and lower than what's represented on this staff, we need a way to notate them. For instance, we know that the lowest note we can play on our bass is E (the open E string), but the lowest note on the staff is G. That's where *ledger lines* come in. Think of ledger lines as a temporary extension of the staff, as needed. The notes continue to progress up or down through the musical alphabet as normal, and we add short lines for each.

G F E A B C D E F G

The 8va and Loco Symbols

The lowest note we can reach on our bass (without the use of alternate tunings or a five- or six-string bass) is the E note found on the first ledger line below the staff. However, we can reach many notes above the staff, and the use of so many ledger lines can be a bit tedious to read. In these instances where we're playing in the upper register of the instrument for an extended period of time, we use the *8va* symbol. This means that any notes affected by it are read as one octave higher.

So, this…

…could be rewritten as this…

…or even this…

To show that the notes are to be read normally again, we use the *loco* symbol.

The bass guitar is actually a *transposing* instrument. This means that when we read notes, we're not playing exactly what's written. We're actually playing notes that are one octave lower than what's written on the page. (The guitar is the same way.) This is done out of convenience, so as to help avoid the use of extensive ledger lines.

Style and Tempo Marking

The "style" portion of this item is fairly self-explanatory. It simply lets the performer know how the song should be played. (For instance, this will prevent a gritty rock song from being played with the sensitivity of a ballad.) The "tempo" portion requires a bit more explanation.

The "Beat"

The Go-Go's had it, but what is it? Perhaps the simplest explanation is this: The beat is what you tap your foot to when you hear music. It's also what you're hearing when someone counts off a tune, as in "1, 2, 3, 4." It's the pulse of the music, and the speed of this pulse is what constitutes the *tempo*.

The tempo is measured in units called *beats per minute* (bpm). So a song with a tempo marking of 60 bpm would have one beat every second, which is a slow tempo. A basic mid-tempo rock song might be approximately 100–120 bpm, a high-energy punk number might be cruising along at 150 bpm or more, and an uptempo be-bop jazz tune could be upwards of 200 bpm.

RHYTHM NOTATION (TIME TO GET YOUR GROOVE ON)

Rhythm is known as one of the three elements of music. The other two, *melody* and *harmony*, are heavily related, but rhythm is sort of on its own. You could hear the notes of the most famous melodies in the world, but if the rhythm is off, those notes may be entirely unrecognizable. Therefore, it's somewhat misleading to say that rhythm makes up one third of music, as the three-element arrangement may suggest. It's almost closer to the truth to say that rhythm constitutes half, while melody and harmony constitute the other half. Regardless of how you slice it, it's safe to say that learning to notate rhythms correctly is an essential music-reading skill.

Time Signature

The *time signature* appears at the beginning of a piece of music, directly after the key signature. Unlike the key signature, which appears on every new staff in the piece, the time signature appears only once, at the very beginning (unless it changes later in the piece, which is relatively uncommon). It consists of two numbers: one on top and one on bottom.

- The **top number** tells you how many beats are in each measure of music.
- The **bottom number** tells you what kind of note gets the beat.

This may sound a little confusing right now, but just hold your horses for a second. It will start to make sense after we clear up a few more things.

By far the most common time signature is 4/4. There are certainly other time signatures, but we'll start with this one for simplicity's sake. First, let's take a look at our basic note values, and then we'll revisit the time signature.

Note Values

Here are the different rhythmic note values that are commonly used.

Whole Note

The whole note is shaped like an empty circle. This note lasts for the entire duration of the measure. In 4/4 time, this note is held for four beats.

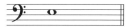

Half Note

The half note is shaped like a whole note, but contains a *stem*. It lasts for half the length of a whole note. (Makes sense, huh?) In 4/4 time, this note is held for two beats.

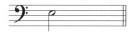

Quarter Note

The quarter note looks like a filled-in half note. It lasts for one quarter of the length of a whole note. (Starting to notice a pattern?) In 4/4 time, this note is held for one beat.

Eighth Note

The eighth note looks like a quarter note, but with a *flag*. No, this doesn't mean it appears mostly in patriotic music. It lasts for one eighth the length of a whole note. In 4/4 time, this note is held for half a beat.

Sixteenth Note

The sixteenth note looks like an eighth note, but with two flags. It lasts for—you guessed it—one sixteenth the length of a whole note. In 4/4 time, this note is held for a fourth of a beat.

As with dynamics (see Chapter 10), this could theoretically go on forever. You'd just simply multiply the note value by two and add another flag each time. Next in line would be the thirty-second note, which would have three flags. The sixty-fourth note would have four flags, etc. Obviously, the smaller the note durations, the less common they are. Sixteenth notes are very common, and thirty-second notes aren't too rare, especially in instrumental solos and the like, but sixty-fourth notes and beyond are far and few between.

The Triplet

Things are getting a little too simple, what with everything being nice and divisible by two, so we need to throw a wrench into things to keep it interesting. Whereas the eighth note divides the beat in half, the triplet divides it into three equal parts. In 4/4 time, this note is held for one third of a beat.

Remember that for every rhythmic note value, there is an equivalent rest symbol. Here, then, are all of the aforementioned note values and their matching rest symbols.

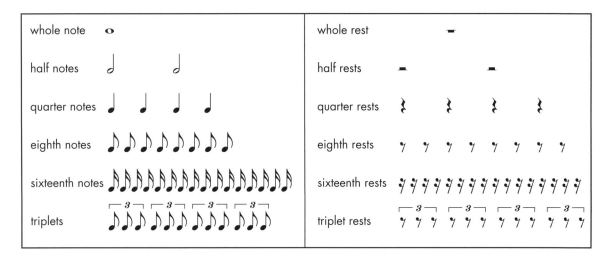

Stems, Beams, and Flags

Earlier we learned that all notes, except for the whole note, have a stem. If you've ever seen much printed music, you may have noticed that stems can point up or down. There is a very simple rule we use when determining stem direction. If the note appears on the middle line of the staff (a D note, remember?) or above, the stem points down. Any note below that (C and below) receives an up-stem.

We also learned that eighth notes, triplets, sixteenth notes, and beyond have added flags to their stems. After writing out a bunch of these, you'd surely realize that it's quite a pain to write all those flags. To make this job easier, we use *beams* when we have more than one of these note values in a row. Think of the beam as one continuous flag that extends to the next note. In 4/4 time, we can beam together up to four eighth notes or four sixteenth notes at a time.

So, this measure of music…

…would actually be written as…

The use of beams will alter stem direction. The rule says that you use the highest or lowest note within the beamed group to determine stem direction for the rest. See the examples below.

As you can see in the top example, it doesn't matter how many low notes there are in a group compared to high ones. The note in the group that's farthest from the middle line determines the stem direction for the whole beamed group.

When the highest and lowest notes are equidistant from the middle line, as in the second example, the stems point down for the beamed group.

Counting Rhythms

In order to keep your place when reading music, it's important that you're able to quickly recognize the different rhythms. Since there are many different rhythmic values used in music, we need ways to make them manageable. This is where *counting* comes in. This is something that you'll need to make a conscious effort to do in the beginning, but it will eventually become second nature (like counting money, for instance).

Let's look at the different note values and how we count them in 4/4 time:

- The **whole note** is held for four beats and is counted as such: **1** (2) (3) (4).
- **Half notes** are held for two beats and are counted as such: **1** (2) **3** (4).
- **Quarter notes** are held for one beat and are counted as such: **1 2 3 4**.
- **Eighth notes** are held for half a beat and are counted as such: **1** & **2** & **3** & **4** &.
- **Sixteenth notes** are held for one fourth of a beat and are counted as such: **1** e & a **2** e & a **3** e & a **4** e & a.
- **Triplets** are held for one third of a beat and are counted as such: **1** & a **2** & a **3** & a **4** & a.

Notice that, in whole notes and half notes, you still count lightly (or silently) on the beats of the measure that you're holding the note. This helps you keep your place throughout each measure.

Now let's listen to all of our rhythmic values in 4/4 time to hear how they actually sound. They'll be played against a metronome "click track" set to a tempo of 80 bpm. Be sure to count along as you play.

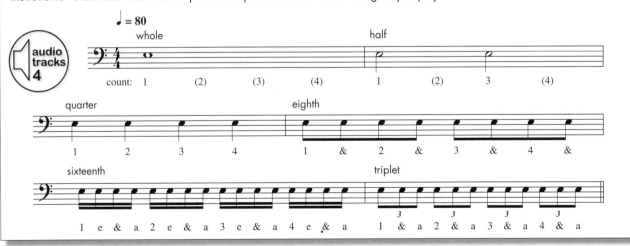

Dots and Ties

There are two special symbols that can be used to alter the rhythmic value of a note: the dot and the tie.

A *tie* combines the value of two notes. When a tie connects two notes, you hold the first note through the rhythmic duration of both notes. (A tie can only be used to connect two notes of the same pitch.)

When a *dot* is placed after a note, it increases its rhythmic value by 50 percent. For example, a dotted quarter note would have the same rhythmic value as a quarter note tied to an eighth note. It's acceptable to use either a dot or a tie. The determining factor is based on convention or personal taste.

Track 5
(0:11)

When reading music, you must be able to count through any rhythm you encounter, so it's a good idea to incorporate this type of exercise into your practice routine: Look at any sheet music and count the rhythm of the notes, disregarding the pitches all together.

Here are a few examples. Don't pay any attention to the pitch of the notes; look only at the rhythms.

The Time Signature (Revisited)

Now that you're familiar with some rhythmic note values, let's take another look at the time signature. We said that each number has a specific purpose, remember? In 4/4, which is the most common time signature, those numbers tell us this:

$\underline{4}$ There are **4 beats** in a measure
4 The **quarter note** receives (is counted as) the beat

Let's look at a few other common time signatures and what they tell us:

$\underline{3}$ There are **3 beats** in a measure
4 The **quarter note** receives the beat

$\underline{6}$ There are **6 beats** in a measure
8 The **eighth note** receives the beat

$\underline{2}$ There are **2 beats** in a measure
2 The **half note** receives the beat

See? And you thought this stuff was complicated!

KEY SIGNATURES (THEY'RE NOT JUST FOR DECORATION!)

As mentioned earlier, the key signature is the first thing that follows the clef on each line of music. It's a collection of sharp (♯) or flat (♭) symbols that lets the performer know what *key* the song is in. Before we get into key signatures, we need to look at these symbols' function.

The Sharp Symbol (♯)

No, you don't need to stay away from these notes for fear of getting pricked. They're no more dangerous than other notes. The sharp symbol tells us to raise a note by the interval of one half step. A *half step* is the smallest distance between two notes in our musical system. This is the same as moving one key on a piano (black or white) or one fret on the bass. For example, if you play the G note at the third fret of string 4, and then play the note at the fourth fret of string 4, you've moved up one half step (G to G♯, in this case).

The Flat Symbol (♭)

The flat symbol is the opposite of the sharp. It tells us to lower the note by the interval of one half step. If you play the G note at the third fret of string 4, and then play the note at the second fret of string 4, you've moved down one half step (G to G♭, in this case).

How Keys Work

Western music is *tonal* music. This means that one note is the centerpiece of a particular song. One note gives the listener the sense of being "at home" or "at rest." This note is known as the *tonic*, and, including sharps and flats, can be any one of 12 notes. This is easiest to see on a piano keyboard. There are seven different white notes before you reach an octave. At various points in between those seven white notes are five different black notes. Seven white notes plus five black notes equal 12 notes total. So there are 12 different keys in music.

Each key uses its own set of seven notes. For instance, the key of C major has no sharps or flats. This is the key you're in if you play nothing but white keys on a piano keyboard. Pianists use the black keys as well (the sharps and/or flats), and that's where the other eleven key signatures come into play (no pun intended!).

When you see a key signature at the beginning of a musical piece, it lets you know which notes you're going to play sharp or flat throughout. For instance, if you see this key signature…

…then you know that every time you come to an F note, you're going to play F♯ instead (one half step higher). Consequently, this would mean that you were in the key of G major. There are 12 different *major keys*, and they all have their own unique key signature. (There are 12 *minor keys* as well, but we'll get into those a bit later.)

Here, then, are the key signatures for each of the 12 major keys. This is something that you'll need to memorize. Don't worry though; there is a logic to it that makes memorization fairly simple.

Notice that, besides C major (which has no sharps or flats), there are two "types" of keys: sharp keys (such as G, D, etc.) and flat keys (such as F, B♭, etc.).

The Circle of 5ths

The circle of 5ths is a great way to learn the 12 key signatures. It arranges the 12 keys in a logical order, making the task of memorization much less intimidating. From the top, the keys progress clockwise around the circle in 5th intervals.

There are two parts of an interval: quantity and quality. To find the *quantity* of an interval, simply count from one note to the next up through the musical alphabet. For example, from C to G is a 5th: C (1)–D (2)–E (3)–F (4)–G (5).

As you progress around the circle to the right (clockwise), one new sharp is added for each key. As you move around the circle in the other direction (counter-clockwise), one new flat is added for each key.

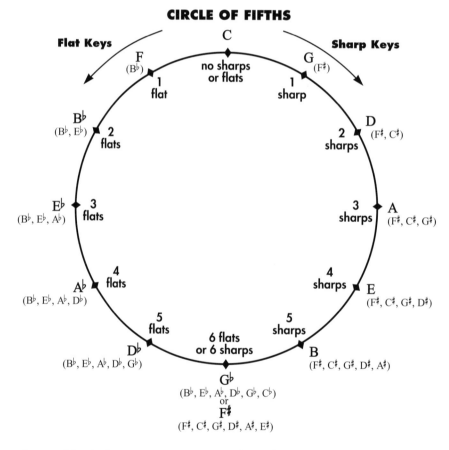

After staring at this circle, you may start to notice a few patterns. (You could also start to zone out, I suppose. But try to stay focused—this is important stuff!) There certainly are many patterns at work here, and they're the keys (again, no pun intended!) to simplifying the memorization process.

On the sharps side, notice that each new key contains the sharps of the previous key plus one more. You may also notice that the sharps themselves progress in the order that the keys appear on the circle when you move clockwise (F♯, C♯, G♯, etc.).

The flats are also cumulatively added, and they, too, appear in the order that the keys appear on the circle (moving counter-clockwise).

Treat this circle as a huge essay question that you know is going to be on a final exam. You need to learn it. It will only take a short while to commit it to memory, and you'll be reaping the benefits for years to come.

Accidentals

When sharps or flats appear in the music in areas other than the key signature, they are known as *accidentals*. These sharp and flat symbols will continue to apply throughout the current measure, so you don't need to re-notate them. However, in the subsequent measure, the notes are once again read as dictated by the key signature.

Take a look at the following examples to see these accidentals in action.

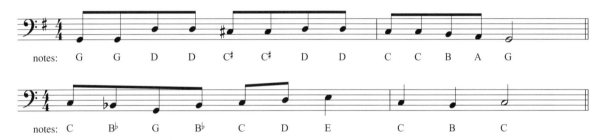

But what about the times when we have a sharp or flat note that we need to be read as a regular note? We have a symbol for that, too, and it's called a natural sign (♮). This symbol tells the performer to temporarily disregard the sharp or flat in the key signature for a specific note. It's also used to cancel out a sharp or flat accidental in the same measure.

Courtesy Accidentals (It's Just Common Courtesy)

Though it's not technically necessary, it's customary to re-notate the proper accidental (as designated by the key signature) in the measure following the temporary accidental. This is called a *courtesy accidental*. It simply reminds the performer of the key signature.

courtesy accidental

courtesy accidental

CHAPTER 5

OTHER FORMS OF NOTATION

What's Ahead:

- Tablature
- Fretboard diagrams
- Chord charts

Standard music notation is extremely useful because it's so universal. A trained musician on any instrument can look at music written for another instrument and usually read it without too much difficulty. This makes it an indispensable tool in your musician arsenal. However, we bassists also make use of other forms of notation. Some of these are forms of shorthand, while others help to more accurately portray the music that's performed on our instrument.

TABLATURE

On some melodic instruments, such as the piano or vibraphone, there is only one place to play one note of a particular octave. If you want to play a C note, there's only one of 12 keys that will produce that note. This is not true of the stringed-instrument family. Bassists, guitarists, violinists, and banjoists can usually play the same note (in the same octave) at several different spots on the neck.

This is where *tablature* comes in handy. Tablature, or "tab," uses four horizontal lines to represent the four strings of the bass. It usually appears in combination with a standard notation staff.

Numbers appear on the lines, indicating what fret to play on what string. There are usually no rhythms used in tab notation, as the rhythm is apparent in the standard-notation staff above.

The figure below tells you to play the G note at fret 3 of the fourth string, play the C note at fret 3 of the third string, and play the D note at fret 5 of the third string.

The main purpose of tablature is to let the performer know exactly where on the neck the notes are played. The same two-measure phrase from the previous figure could be played a number of ways on the bass. Here are a few:

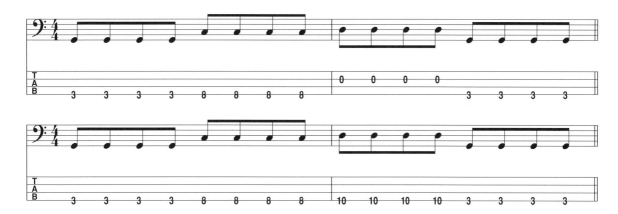

The same note will sound slightly different when played on different strings of the bass. The thicker strings will produce a "boomier" or "rounder" tone, while the thinner strings produce a "punchier," more "focused" sound. Here is the same A note played at four different spots on the bass:

So, with the use of tablature, we will know exactly where on the fretboard a bass line was played and, in the process, be sure to get the right tone.

The History of Tab

Tablature is by no means a new development. In fact, it's been around since the Renaissance period, where it was created to notate music on fretted instruments of the time. The most popular of these instruments was the *lute*. Lutes were (and still are) made of nearly all wood and featured a rounded back and a tear-shaped body. The frets were made from tying loops of gut around the neck and would have to be replaced after extensive use.

FRETBOARD DIAGRAMS

A *fretboard diagram* is a handy little tool used to quickly plot out certain notes on the bass. It's perhaps used most for notating scale and arpeggio shapes (see Chapters 6 & 7). Though at first glance they may look like an empty spreadsheet document, the grid-like appearance is actually representative of your bass's neck.

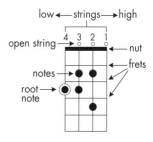

The long vertical lines represent the strings, while the shorter horizontal lines represent the frets. (Fretboard diagrams usually show five frets, but they can show more or less, as needed.) A dark, thick line at the top represents the nut. The circles indicate the notes to play. If it's a scale or arpeggio, the root note is often circled.

In instances where you're showing areas of the neck other than the first five frets, the nut is removed and in its place is a position marker to let you know the location. In this diagram, frets 5 through 9 are shown. Therefore, you would be playing in fifth position.

Position is determined by the location of your first finger on the fretboard. If your first finger is playing a note at fret 7, then you are in "seventh position."

These diagrams make no mention of melody or rhythm. They simply tell you where the notes of a particular scale, riff, or arpeggio are found on the neck. To this end, they are occasionally used in place of tab to indicate where on the neck the notes of a phrase are played, such as in the following example. Here, the diagram tells you to play the A note at fret 5 of the fourth string, the C note at fret 8 of the fourth string, and so on.

CHORD CHARTS

A *chord chart* is perhaps the least specific of all forms of notation. Here, a staff is often used, but typically only for showing the division of measures. Chord symbols appear above the staff to let you know what harmony is sounding at what time in the song. When reading from a chord chart, it's left up to you to improvise your own bass line, based off the chords of the song. After you're through with this book, you'll be able to do just that!

Here are a couple of examples of chord charts:

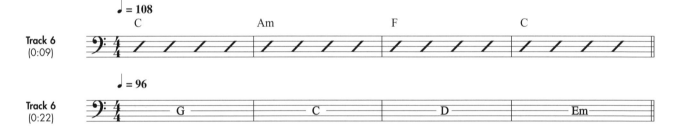

Occasionally, a skeletal rhythm is depicted in such a chart. This is usually during one measure, at a point in the song where there is an obvious rhythmic accent the entire band is supposed to hit. In the following chart, it's left up to you for the first two measures. However, in measure 3 the band is going to join in for a D7–A ensemble figure on beats 1 and 2, and they're going to do it with or without you. So you may as well join in on the fun! The rest on beats 3 and 4 tells you to lay out for the remainder of the measure.

CHAPTER 6
SCALES, SCALES, SCALES

What's Ahead:
- Major and minor scale shapes
- Relative and parallel minor concepts

Scales. The mere word sends chills throughout the spines of musicians everywhere. Well, I'm happy to inform you that there's nothing to fear. Scales are your friend—really. In Chapter 4, we began to learn about keys and the concept of *tonal* music. If you made it through that chapter without throwing, ripping, or burning this book, then congratulations—you've made it through the most difficult part. All of these seemingly random bits of information that you've been asked to store should all start to come together and make sense now. Here, we're going to take a look at perhaps the most important bit of music theory you'll ever learn: the **major scale**.

> A *scale* is a collection of notes (usually seven) that together suggest a certain tonality, or mood. Some scales sound happy, some sound sad, while others can sound wicked, bluesy, or mysterious.

THE MAJOR SCALE

The major scale is by far the most commonly used scale in Western music. It's a seven-note scale with a specific formula of whole steps and half steps that results in a very consonant, pleasing sound.

> Whole steps and half steps are musical *intervals*. (We learned earlier that an interval is the distance between two notes.) On the bass guitar, a whole step is the distance of two frets on the same string (from fret 3 to fret 5, for example). A half step, as we learned earlier, is half of that—the distance of one fret on the same string (from fret 3 to fret 4, for example).

Construction: Building Your Very Own Major Scale

A major scale is built off the following formula with regard to whole and half steps:

whole–whole–half–whole–whole–whole–half

Repeat this formula again and again. Make up a little song with it, if you'd like. This is a very important formula, and it *will* be on the final exam!

So, to construct a major scale in any key, all you do is pick a root note (tonic) and follow the aforementioned formula. You'll end up with a major scale in the key of your root. Let's give it a shot. We'll start with a C major scale.

Wait a minute! The major scale is supposed to be a seven-note scale, but there are eight notes here. Well, yes, there are eight notes here, but there are only seven *different* notes. The last note is another C, at which point the scale would start over in a new octave.

The root note, or tonic, of a scale is the note that gives the strongest sense of resolution. Oftentimes, if a song is in the key of C, the melody will end on a C note. Many melodies move away from the tonic in specific ways and then resolve to the tonic at the end, creating a sense of "returning home" or "coming to rest."

Playing the Major Scale

Now let's see how this could be played on the bass. While it's not the most practical method, it's usually easiest to see the formula in action by playing the scale on one string. This way, the arrangement of whole and half steps is easy to grasp. Here's the C major scale played entirely on the third string.

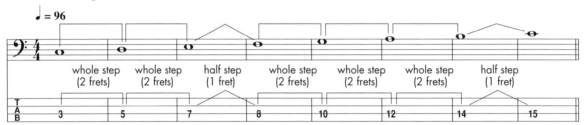

By scaling one string, the pattern of whole and half steps is easily identified. However, this method is not very practical for playing purposes. We have more than one string on our bass, so we may as well make use of them. We can finger this scale with much less effort by remaining in one position. Here are the same notes, but this time we'll remain in second position throughout.

Track 7
(0:24)

Since we're in "second position," our first finger is on fret 2. So, in the previous scale, your first finger plays all the notes on fret 2, your second finger handles the notes on fret 3, your third finger gets the note on fret 4, and your fourth finger plays all the notes on fret 5.

Notice that no sharps or flats were needed in this scale. This is because, if you remember from Chapter 4, the key of C major has no sharps or flats.

The musical alphabet has two half steps built into it: between B and C and between E and F. This is why C major needs no sharps or flats; the half steps are already built into the scale. This is also why there are seven different white notes and five different black notes within an octave on a piano keyboard. If you think of the seven white keys as the "natural" notes and the five black keys as the "accidental" notes, this makes perfect sense. There are two sets of white keys that don't have black ones in between them: B–C and E–F.

OK. Are you ready for a new key? When dealing with any other major key besides C, we're going to have to add either sharps or flats. If we follow our major scale formula, it will tell us which notes need to be sharped or flatted. Let's try G major.

If we follow the major-scale formula, we see that we're going to need one accidental in this scale: F will need to be raised to F♯.

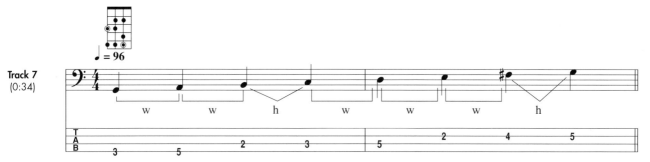

Flip back to the Circle of 5ths in Chapter 4 and take a look at G major. It has one sharp in its key signature: F♯. You see! You weren't doing this for your health. There is logic to this music-theory stuff. So if you were to rewrite the G major scale with a key signature instead of an accidental, it would look like this:

That F♯ in the key signature tells us to raise every F note we see to F♯ throughout the song. Let's look at one more key: F major. When starting from F, we'll find that we'll need to add a flat to B. We're supposed to have a half step from the 3rd to the 4th note, but A (3rd) to B (4th) is a whole step. Therefore, we make the B note a B♭, and all is well.

A quick glance at the Circle of 5ths confirms that F major has one flat (B♭) in its key signature. So our F major scale written with a key signature would look like this:

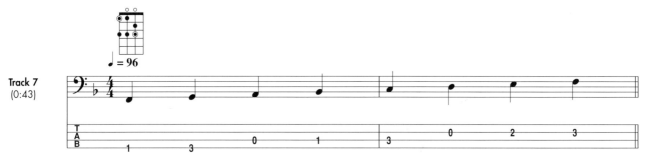

Hopefully, you're beginning to notice a pattern in these major scales—in your left hand at least. They all have the same shape on the fretboard. (F major uses open strings, but if you think of those open strings as fret "0," you should see the similar pattern.) This means that the scale shape is movable to any key. All you have to do is move the whole shape to a new root note, and you're playing a major scale in a different key. Here, then, are all the 12 major scales shown in diagram form. Listen to Track 8 for a demonstration of the first six scales.

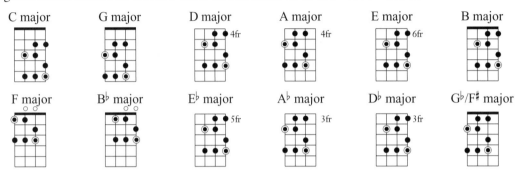

When practicing these scales, use a metronome. This will help you simultaneously work on your timing as well as your right- and left-hand coordination. Also, practice the scales by starting from the top note as well as starting from the bottom note.

Melodies That Use the Major Scale

Are you ready to put your newfound music-reading skills to work? Let's take a look at some classic melodies that are constructed from the major scale. Practice each one slowly until you can play through the whole song at an even tempo.

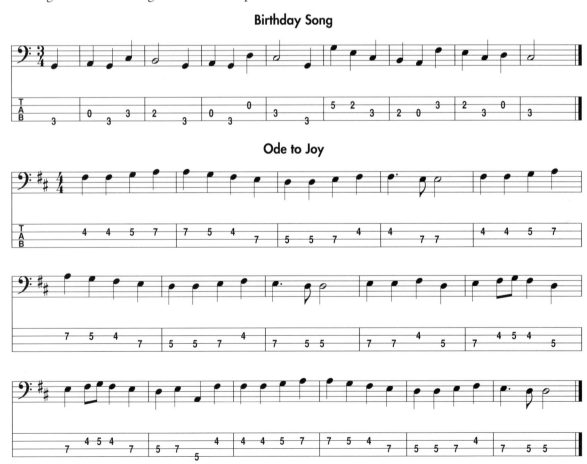

Amazing Grace

When the Saints Go Marching In

THE MINOR SCALE

So far, we've learned a good deal about major keys and scales, and it's now time to turn to the dark side: minor keys. The minor scale (also known as the natural minor scale) is another seven-note scale that's very common in Western music. It contains a different formula of whole and half steps than the major scale, and the resulting sound is usually described as dark or sad. If the major scale is Luke Skywalker, the minor scale is Darth Vader.

Construction: Different Ballpark, Same City

When we look at the scale formulas for scales other than the major scale, we usually don't refer to it in whole and half steps. Rather, we use a numerical formula in relation to the major scale. The major-scale notes are numbered 1–2–3–4–5–6–7. When we look at other scales, we use this numerical system, but alter certain numbers to create other scale formulas.

For example, the scale formula for a minor scale is 1–2–♭3–4–5–♭6–♭7. This means that a minor scale contains the same notes as a major scale, but the 3rd, 6th, and 7th notes (or scale *degrees*) are lowered one half step.

C major scale

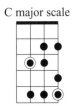

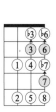

C minor scale

Playing the Minor Scale

Since we like to finger scales in the most comfortable position possible, the minor scale is usually re-fingered as such:

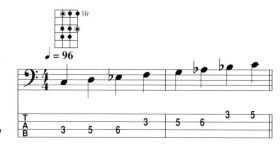

Relative Minor and Parallel Minor

There are two ways in which we relate minor scales to major scales: *relative minor* and *parallel minor*. Relative and parallel minors are two very different things. In short, the difference is this:

- **Relative minors** share the same key signature with their major counterparts.
- **Parallel minors** share the same root with their major counterparts.

We just dealt with a parallel minor: a C major scale was transformed into a C minor scale. This is a parallel-minor relationship; C minor is the parallel minor of C major. They both share the same root (C).

A relative minor will not have the same root, but it will contain exactly the same notes and, therefore, the same key signature. We find a major scale's relative minor by starting and ending the scale from/at the 6th degree. For example, if we have the same C major scale again, we can find its relative minor by counting up the scale to 6: C (1)–D (2)–E (3)–F (4)–G (5)–A (6). A is the 6th tone. So, A minor is the relative minor of C major.

A minor

Let's take a look at the Circle of 5ths again, but this time we'll add the minor keys, as well. Every major key has a relative minor (located on the inside of the circle) that shares its key signature. A lowercase "m" after a note name is the symbol for minor.

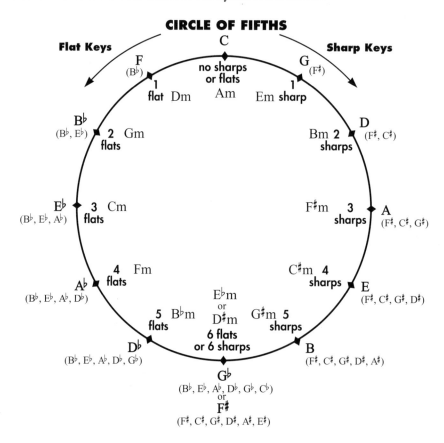

CIRCLE OF FIFTHS

Melodies That Use the Minor Scale

Now let's play a few melodies that make use of minor scales. Remember to play slowly at first, if needed. It's *always* better to play something consistently slow than to plow through parts of it and trip up on other parts.

Sometimes I Feel Like a Motherless Child

Joshua (Fit the Battle of Jericho)

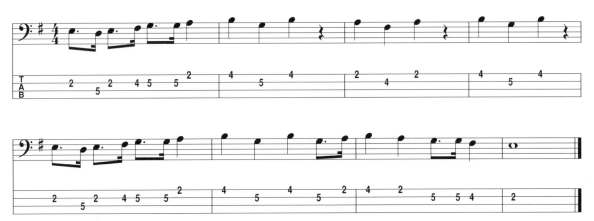

CHAPTER 7
CHORDS AND ARPEGGIOS: WHEN SCALES AREN'T ENOUGH

What's Ahead:

- Intervals and basic scale/chord theory
- Major and minor arpeggio shapes

ALL ABOUT INTERVALS

Before we jump into chords and arpeggios, we need to take a closer look at *intervals*. We've come across a few of these already, such as the octave, the 4th (in tuning), the whole step, and the half step. All of these are intervals. We learned earlier that intervals have two parts: quality and quantity. Quantity, as we now know, is simply determined by counting from note to note. Now we're going to look at *quality*.

So what do we mean by quality? Are some intervals better than others? Do some come with money-back guarantees? No, no. The quality of an interval further defines it by attaching one of five distinguishing labels: major, minor, perfect, augmented, or diminished. When labeling intervals, we use the following symbols: M = major, m = minor, P = perfect, A = augmented, d = diminished.

Now, here's the tricky part. Not any interval can be any quality. They're organized as follows:

- 2nds, 3rds, and 6ths   are usually   major or minor
- 4ths and 5ths   can be   perfect, augmented, or diminished
- 7ths   are usually   major, minor, or diminished
- Octaves   are always   perfect

Major and Perfect Intervals

The major and perfect intervals are easiest to start with because they're all present in a major scale. If you measure the distance from the root of a major scale to any other note in the scale, you're always going to get either a major interval or a perfect interval.

Let's look at the C major scale (C–D–E–F–G–A–B–C):

- From C to D is a major 2nd.
- From C to E is a major 3rd.
- From C to F is a perfect 4th.
- From C to G is a perfect 5th.
- From C to A is a major 6th.
- From C to B is a major 7th.
- From C to C is a perfect octave.

Here's how these intervals sound on the bass. Try playing the two notes together and then separately.

| (M2) Major 2nd | (M3) Major 3rd | (P4) Perfect 4th | (P5) Perfect 5th | (M6) Major 6th | (M7) Major 7th | (P8) Perfect Octave |

      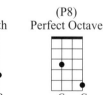

4ths, 5ths, and octaves will never be major or minor.

Another way to look at intervals is by measuring them in half steps. Let's take a look at the aforementioned intervals in terms of half steps.

- A major 2nd is two half steps.
- A major 3rd is four half steps.
- A perfect 4th is five half steps.
- A perfect 5th is seven half steps.

- A major 6th is nine half steps.
- A major 7th is eleven half steps.
- A perfect octave is 12 half steps.

Minor Intervals

Now that you're familiar with major intervals, minor intervals are easy. Any major interval is made minor by closing the distance one half step. In other words, if C to D is a major 2nd, then C to D♭ is a minor 2nd. See below:

C to D = M2 $\longrightarrow$ C to D♭ = m2
C to E = M3 $\longrightarrow$ C to E♭ = m3
C to A = M6 $\longrightarrow$ C to A♭ = m6
C to B = M7 $\longrightarrow$ C to B♭ = m7

- A minor 2nd is one half step.
- A minor 3rd is three half steps.
- A minor 6th is eight half steps.
- A minor 7th is ten half steps.

Let's hear these minor intervals on the bass.

Track 10
(0:40)

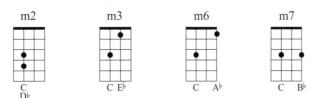

Augmented and Diminished Intervals

Augmented and diminished intervals work in a similar way as major and minor intervals and relate directly to perfect intervals.

- When a perfect interval is **raised one half step**, it is an **augmented** interval.
- When a perfect interval is **lowered one half step**, it is a **diminished** interval.

C to F = P4 $\longrightarrow$ C to F♯ = A4
C to G = P5 $\longrightarrow$ C to G♯ = A5 $\longrightarrow$ C to G♭ = d5

- An augmented 4th is six half steps.
- An augmented 5th is eight half steps.
- A diminished 5th is six half steps.

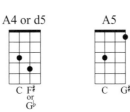

Track 10
(1:05)

Now let's hear how these sound.

Wait a minute—what happened to the diminished 4th? Technically, a diminished 4th (e.g., C to F♭) is possible, but its equivalent, the major 3rd (F♭ = E), is more commonly used. You may have also noticed that an augmented 4th is the same thing as a diminished 5th; both are six half steps. This interval, which divides the octave directly in half, is known as the tritone, as it's constructed of three whole steps.

> When two of the same notes have a different name, they are said to be *enharmonic*. For example, G♭ and F♯ are both the same note, so they are enharmonic. There is a theory for which name is used at which time, but it is, for the most part, beyond the scope of this book.

You may have also noticed that the augmented 5th interval (eight half steps) is the same distance as the minor 6th interval. The only way to tell intervals of this kind apart is by the note name. If there are six note names involved (C to A♭), the interval is called a minor 6th. If there are five note names involved (C to G♯), it's called an augmented 5th.

There are a few other instances when you'll see augmented or diminished intervals. These include augmented 2nds and diminished 7ths. We'll see where they come into play a bit later.

Here, then, are all 12 intervals measured in half steps and their most common name:

Number of half steps	Interval name	Number of half steps	Interval name
1	m2	7	P5
2	M2	8	m6
3	m3	9	M6
4	M3	10	m7
5	P4	11	M7
6	A4 or d5	12	P8

CHORDS

The basic definition of a chord is: three or more notes played simultaneously. "Any three notes?" you ask? Well, technically, yes—any three notes constitute a chord. However, by far the most common three-note chord is the *triad*. The triad is the basis for harmony in countless compositions, from the latest pop hit to the classical masterpieces of the past.

The Triad

The triad is a chord that contains a root, a 3rd, and a 5th. There are four types of triads: **major**, **minor**, **augmented**, and **diminished**. (You should recognize these names from our interval study earlier. If you don't, you must not have been paying attention!) Each one has its own unique intervallic construction.

Major Triads

A major triad contains a root, a major 3rd, and a perfect 5th. In other words, you have a root note, a note four half steps away, and another note seven half steps away. You can build a triad off of any root note. For example, a C major triad would contain the notes C, E, and G.

C to E is a 3rd because three note names are involved: C (1)–D (2)–E (3). It's a *major* 3rd because it's four half steps: C^C♯^D^D♯^E.

C to G is a 5th because five note names are involved: C (1)–D (2)–E (3)–F (4)–G (5). It's a *perfect* 5th because it's seven half steps: C^C♯^D^D♯^E^F^F♯^G.

There are two natural half steps in the musical alphabet. These lie between B and C and between E and F.

F major would be spelled F–A–C:

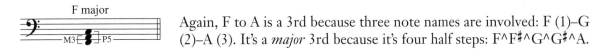

Again, F to A is a 3rd because three note names are involved: F (1)–G (2)–A (3). It's a *major* 3rd because it's four half steps: F^F♯^G^G♯^A.

F to C is a 5th because five note names are involved: F (1)–G (2)–A (3)–B (4)–C (5). It's a *perfect* fifth because it's seven half steps: F^F♯^G^G♯^A^A♯^B^C.

When you see a chord symbol with nothing else attached to it, a major triad is implied. So when you see the chord symbols C, F, and G, this means C major, F major, and G major. All other types of triads (chords) will have something else attached to the chord symbol to further differentiate it.

If we build a major triad off of D, we'll need to include an accidental: F♯. D to F♯ is a 3rd because three note names are involved: D (1)–E (2)–F♯ (3). It's a *major* 3rd because it's four half steps: D^D♯^E^F^F♯. This is why we need the F♯. D to F is only a minor 3rd (three half steps). But we need a major 3rd to make a major triad, so we have to raise F to F♯.

D to A is a 5th because five note names are involved: D (1)–E (2)–F♯ (3)–G (4)–A (5). It's a *perfect* 5th because it's seven half steps: D^D♯^E^F^F♯^G^G♯^A.

Here, then, are all 12 major triads and their spellings:

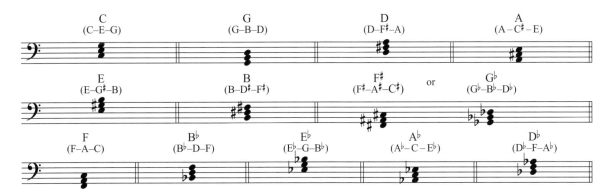

Minor Triads

A minor triad contains a root and a perfect 5th, just like the major triad. However, instead of a major 3rd, it contains a—you guessed it—*minor* 3rd. Major triad = happy; minor triad = sad. Got it? OK, good.

So to make our C major triad (C–E–G) a C minor triad, all we need to do is lower the 3rd by a half step. We end up with C–E♭–G.

To make a D major triad (D–F♯–A) a D minor triad, we need to lower the 3rd (F♯) a half step to F.

You see? This is easy. Here are all 12 minor triads and their spelling. If you compare these with the major triads, you'll find that only the 3rd has been lowered a half step in every instance.

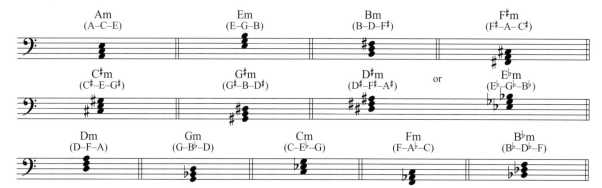

Augmented Triads

Augmented triads are similar to major triads in that they have a major 3rd. However, instead of a perfect 5th, augmented triads have an augmented 5th. (Makes sense, huh?) So to make a C major triad (C–E–G) a C augmented triad, we just raise the 5th by one half step (C–E–G♯).

We say G♯ and not A♭ in this instance because the interval is a 5th (augmented, in this case). If we used A♭, that would make the interval a minor 6th.

The chord symbol for an augmented triad consists of a "+" after the note name. So the chord symbol for C augmented is simply "C+." Here, then, are all 12 augmented triads. Compare these with the major triads and you'll find that only the 5th has been raised a half step in each instance.

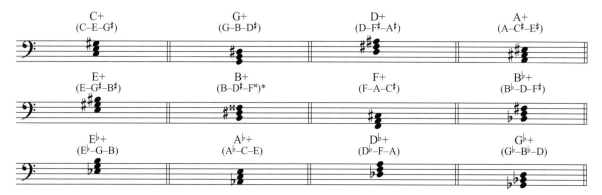

*The "×" symbol means "double-sharp." F× (read: "F double-sharp") is the same note as G, but in a B+ chord it's technically called F× because it's an augmented 5th interval. B to G would be a minor 6th.

Diminished Triads

Diminished triads are similar to minor triads in that they have a minor 3rd. However, instead of a perfect 5th, they have a diminished 5th. So to make a C minor triad (C–E♭–G) a C diminished triad, we just lower the 5th by one half step (C–E♭–G♭).

The chord symbol for a diminished triad consists of a "o" symbol after the note name. So the chord symbol for C diminished is simply "C°." Next, then, are all 12 diminished triads. Compare these with the minor triads and you'll find that only the 5th has been lowered a half step in each instance.

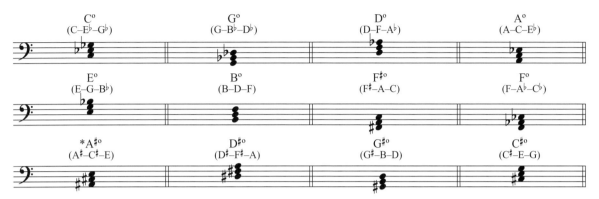

*To avoid the use of double-flats ($\flat\flat$), A$^{\sharp\circ}$, D$^{\sharp\circ}$, G$^{\sharp\circ}$, and C$^{\sharp\circ}$ are enharmonic spellings of B$^{\flat\circ}$, E$^{\flat\circ}$, A$^{\flat\circ}$, and D$^{\flat\circ}$, respectively.

The 7th Chord

While the triad contains three notes, the seventh chord contains four notes. It's the second most popular type of chord used in popular music (except in jazz, where it's more popular than the triad). We form seventh chords by stacking another note on top of the triad—a 7th interval. So a seventh chord will have a root, 3rd, 5th, and 7th.

There are many different types of seventh chords, but here we're going to concentrate on the most common: **major 7th**, **minor 7th**, **dominant 7th**, **minor 7$\flat$5**, and **diminished 7th**.

Major 7th

The major 7th chord is the brightest-sounding one of all. It's created by placing a major 7th interval on top of a major triad. It contains a root, major 3rd, perfect 5th, and major 7th.

The chord symbol for a major seventh chord consists of "maj7" after the note name. So the chord symbol for C major 7th is simply "Cmaj7." Here are all 12 major 7th chords and their spellings.

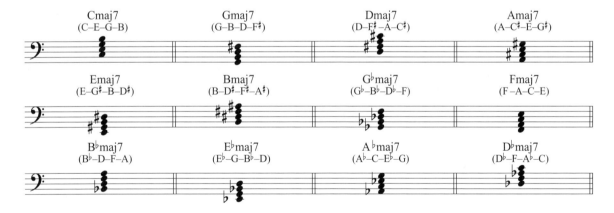

Minor 7th

The minor 7th chord is created by placing a minor 7th interval on top of a minor triad. It contains the root, minor 3rd, perfect 5th, and minor 7th.

The chord symbol for a minor 7th chord consists of "m7" after the note name. So the chord symbol for C minor 7th is simply "Cm7." Next are all 12 minor 7th chords and their spellings.

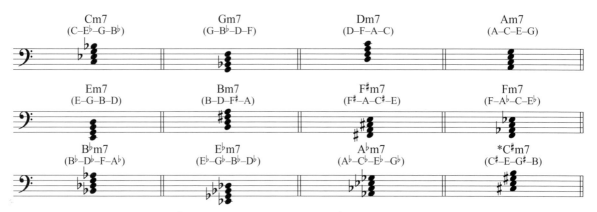

*To avoid the use of double-flats, C♯m7 is an enharmonic spelling of D♭m7.

Dominant 7th

The dominant 7th chord has a bluesy sound to it and is created by placing a minor 7th interval on top of a major triad. It contains the root, major 3rd, perfect 5th, and minor 7th.

The chord symbol for a dominant 7th chord consists of "7" after the note name. So the chord symbol for C dominant 7th is simply "C7." Here are all 12 dominant 7th chords and their spellings.

Minor 7♭5

The minor 7♭5 chord is created by placing a minor 7th interval on top of a diminished triad. It contains the root, minor 3rd, diminished 5th, and minor 7th and is sometimes referred to as a half-diminished chord.

The chord symbol for a minor 7♭5 chord consists of "m7♭5" after the note name. So the chord symbol for C minor 7♭5 is simply "Cm7♭5." Here are all 12 minor 7♭5 chords and their spellings.

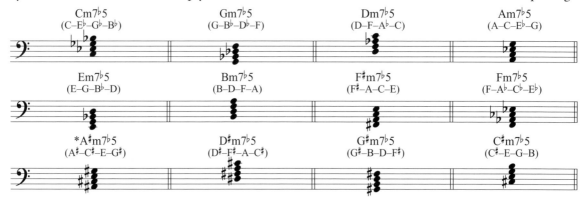

*To avoid the use of double-flats, A♯m7♭5, D♯m7♭5, G♯m7♭5, and C♯m7♭5 are enharmonic spellings of B♭m7♭5, E♭m7♭5, A♭m7♭5, and D♭m7♭5, respectively.

Diminished 7th

The diminished 7th chord is created by placing a *diminished* 7th interval on top of a diminished triad. (A diminished 7th interval is one half step smaller than a minor 7th.) It contains the root, minor 3rd, diminished 5th, and diminished 7th and is sometimes referred to as a fully diminished chord.

The chord symbol for a diminished 7th chord consists of "°7" after the note name. So the chord symbol for C diminished 7th is simply "C°7." Here are all 12 diminished 7th chords and their spellings.

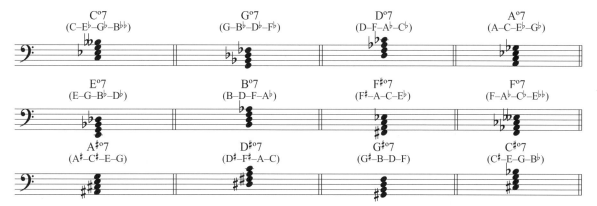

ARPEGGIOS (MORE THAN JUST A FANCY ITALIAN WORD)

OK, it may have occurred to you at some point during our chord studies that… you're a bass player, and you don't play chords! While this is true, there is a good reason why bass players need to understand how chords are constructed. That reason is the arpeggio.

An *arpeggio* is simply the notes of a chord played one at a time (melodically) instead of simultaneously (harmonically). While we rarely play chords, we can make great use of arpeggios in our bass lines. Let's take a look at how we can play them on the bass. Several fingering options are given for each arpeggio; all the forms are moveable to any root note.

> The forms that only occupy three consecutive strings can be moved up a string group, as well. For instance, if a form makes use of strings 4, 3, and 2, that same form can be shifted to the 3–2–1 string group, and vice versa.

Triad Arpeggios

The notes of a triad arpeggio are used in bass lines of many different musical styles, including rock, country, jazz, and blues, among others. Knowing these forms inside and out is essential to opening up your options on the bass and getting out of the "root rut."

Major Triad

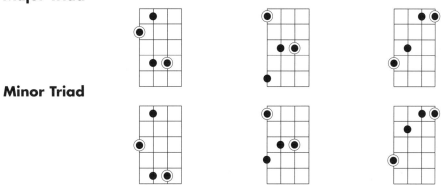

Minor Triad

Augmented Triad

Diminished Triad

7th-Chord Arpeggios

Seventh-chord arpeggios are extremely useful in blues and jazz styles, as well as funk and, to an extent, rock. Some major light bulbs should start to go off when you look at certain bass lines after you're familiar with these shapes.

Major 7th

Minor 7th

Dominant 7th

Minor 7♭5

Diminished 7th

CHAPTER 8
THE ROLE OF THE BASS

> ***What's Ahead:***
> - What does a bassist do?
> - Common approaches to writing bass lines

Imagine, if you will, a world without the bass. You'd have nothing to make your head bob side to side during a country tune. You could pretty much kiss funk goodbye. You'd never experience that spine-tingling sensation of your very frame coming unglued as the constant barrage of low frequencies rattled your skeleton. Suffice it to say, the bass has become an indispensable link in the musical chain. In this chapter, we're going to look at how and why bassists do what we do.

YOUR PRIMARY OBJECTIVES

What's your motivation? Why are you here? Why is anyone here? What were we talking about, again? Oh, yes, bass players. Just as it would be criminally simplistic to reduce a drummer's function to "keeping time," it's impossible to sum up a bass player's role with one phrase, as well. The bass plays a significant part in many aspects of a band's sound, and the area of focus shifts slightly with each style. However, there are a few fundamental concepts at the core of our existence, and we'll look at those now.

Harmonic Foundation

While the guitars and keyboards often fill out the harmony with chords and/or fills, we bassists are usually responsible for sounding the root. Of course, we play much more than root notes, but it's often the bass that gives a chord progression its punch. When people hum something in a song other than the vocal melody, it's often the bass line.

Establishing a Groove

Along with the drummer, a bassist is largely the one responsible for the groove of the song. Whether it's busy, laid back, relentless and driving, or full-tilt swinging, we see to it that the groove is well taken care of. This is accomplished with a wide range of rhythmic and melodic approaches.

Keeping the Beat

Another duty shared with the drums, we often provide the rock-solid beat that keeps the heads bobbin' and the booties shakin' out on the dance floor. Oftentimes, the bass guitar and the kick drum function as one unit, clearly defining where the song's beat falls.

WRITING BASS LINES: DOS AND DON'TS—ACTUALLY, JUST DOS

There are many ways to approach a bass line. There are no rules, really—perhaps just conventions. And if there were rules, well… you know what they say about rules. This is why there really aren't any "don'ts" here. The bass guitar has no boundaries, except for that of your imagination. And while there are a few tried-and-true methods that have become popular, in the end, the sky's the limit.

Having said that, let's get you started with a few "can't miss" approaches.

The Root Note

You can't get any more simplistic and straightforward than chugging away on root notes. Yet, there are some songs in which this approach fits the bill perfectly. Many a bass line has been built on roots played in steady eighth notes—and if it ain't broke, don't fix it!

Sometimes an *approach tone* is used to spice up things a bit. This can be an accented tone that falls on the downbeat, or it can appear as a lead-in, just before the downbeat. Common approach tones are half steps and whole steps below the root note.

The Root and 5th

The 5th can be added to the root for more melodic interest. The 5th can either be played above the root (a 5th up) or below the root (a 4th down). This approach is an old standby in country music.

The higher octave of the root is often brought in for added interest, as well.

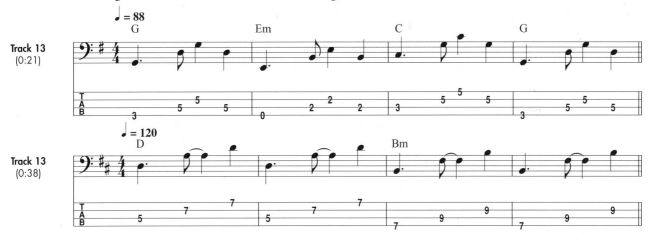

With a little rhythmic *syncopation*, you can come up with some funky lines using only these notes.

To *syncopate* means to place the accent on the weak part of the beat. The downbeats (what you tap your feet to) are usually accented by default, but when you accent the spots in between, you're making use of syncopation—a very powerful rhythmic device, which we'll explore in further detail later on.

Arpeggiation

We already talked about using the 5th in conjunction with the root. When we add the 3rd to those notes, we've moved into the realm of the arpeggio. This technique further expands your note options and will help to clearly outline the harmony if you're playing without a chordal instrument, such as a guitar or keyboard.

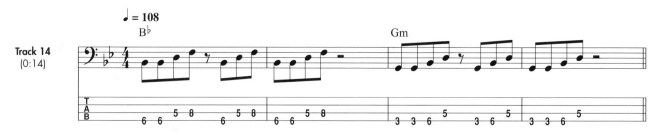

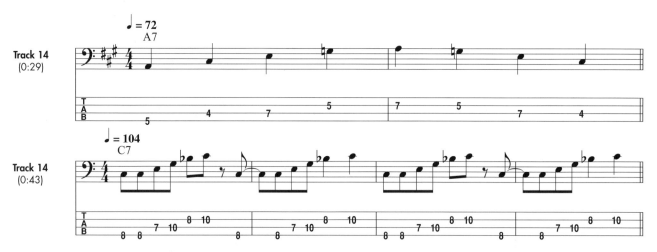

Our seventh-chord arpeggios can be used as well, especially in blues.

Other Common Devices

There are many other ways to spice up our lines (besides eating some Cajun food before you play!). Let's take a look at a few.

Passing Tones

A *passing tone* is a non-chord tone (a note that's not part of the chord) that's used to connect two other chord tones. These can be either *diatonic* (found in the song's key) or *chromatic* (a half step—usually outside the key). These tones provide a smooth transition between roots. The passing tones are labeled in these next examples: D.P.T. = diatonic passing tone, C.P.T. = chromatic passing tone.

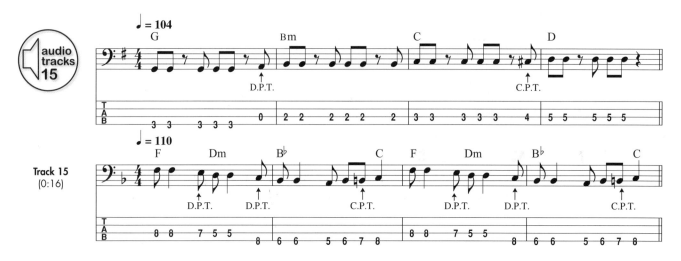

Scalar Runs

Sometimes a brief run through part of a scale can add a nice lift to a line. The scale used is most often the major or minor scale of the key, but it can be others, as well. Use your ear to judge what sounds best.

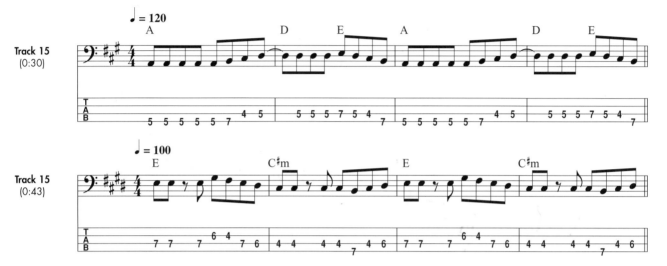

Octave Transference

Sometimes simply repeating part of the line in a different octave can make all the difference in the world. Bringing something down an octave can create a sense of fullness or weight, while moving into the higher octave can generate excitement.

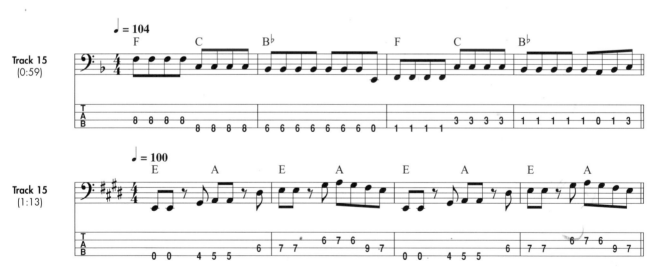

LEARN FROM THE PROS!

Now let's take a look at some of these concepts being put to use by real pros. You'll notice that in real musical situations, many of these concepts are combined to make one interesting yet functional bass line.

Killing Floor

Words and Music by
Chester Burnett

Moderate Rock ♩ = 120

A7

Dancing in the Street

Words and Music by Marvin Gaye,
Ivy Hunter and William Stevenson

Moderately ♩ = 114

E7

Paperback Writer

Words and Music by
John Lennon and Paul McCartney

Moderately fast Rock ♩ = 166

G

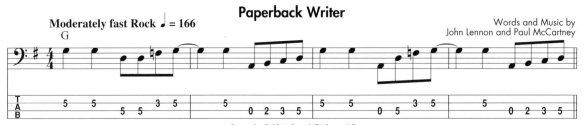

Smells Like Teen Spirit

Words and Music by Kurt Cobain,
Krist Novoselic and Dave Grohl

Moderate Rock ♩ = 114

N.C. (F5)   (B♭5)   (A♭5)   (D♭5)

Another One Bites the Dust

Words and Music by
John Deacon

Moderate Rock ♩ = 110

N.C. (Em)   (Am)   (Em)   (Am)

Getting a Feel for the Groove

CHAPTER 9

SETTLING INTO YOUR NEW HOME: THE RHYTHM SECTION

> **What's Ahead:**
> * Finding your place in the rhythm section
> * Decorating your new home with subtle touches (additional techniques)

As a bass player, you're officially part of an elite organization known as the *rhythm section*. Though this term can refer to any rhythm instrument (e.g., guitar, keys), it typically refers to the bass and drums. The drummer is going to become your new best friend (whether you like it or not!).

GETTING FAMILIAR WITH THE DRUM KIT

There are several key elements of the drum kit that you need to be tuned in to when playing together. By accentuating different elements, you can achieve a wide variety of different feels and grooves.

The Bass Drum (Kick Drum)

This is the biggest drum of the kit—the one sitting on the floor that the drummer plays with his foot. It provides the punch and thump to the beat and oftentimes lets the listener know where beat 1 is located.

One common approach is for the bass guitar and kick drum to act as one unit. The bass plays right along with the kick and provides a pitch to its thump. This will give a punchy, solid feel and is always a great option when you don't have time to write a fancy line.

Here's how this approach sounds. Note that this approach can consist of root notes only or other tones, as well.

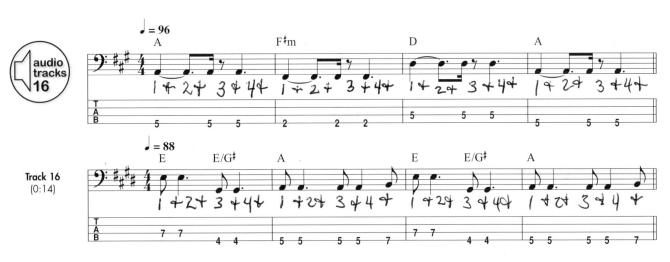

Track 16
(0:14)

We can create an entirely different feel by playing around the kick drum (i.e., not always in sync with it). Listen to the grooves below. The bass carves out more of its own space and adds another dimension to the groove.

Notice how this achieves an entirely different effect than playing with the kick. It may not always be the sound you're looking for, but sometimes it's best to try out both approaches and see what works.

Of course, the previous examples represent the two extremes. There are a million variations between the two that are also fair game! However, putting yourself within certain parameters, as in the previous examples, can sometimes help you to create lines that you may have never otherwise considered.

The Hi-hat

The hi-hat (or "hat") is the most prominent time-keeper of the drum set. It's usually played in a consistent eighth- or sixteenth-note pattern, and, therefore, provides the steady clicking sound that keeps the beat in line. As with the kick, there are different ways you can adjust your lines in relation to the hi-hat to achieve different feels.

Many times a bassist will use the hi-hat rhythm as a basis for the rhythmic feel of the bass line. In other words, if the hi-hat is playing sixteenth notes, we can follow suit by playing sixteenth note–based lines. For an eighth-note pattern, we use an eighth-note feel. This results in a uniform sound and a steady, tight groove. Check out the following examples:

* This indicates a sixteenth-note swing feel. It's essentially the same concept as the eighth-note shuffle, but the sixteenth notes are affected instead of the eighths (see Chapter 10).

By using an opposing rhythmic approach, we can really shake things up. Using sixteenths over an eighth-note hi-hat pattern can add real excitement, while eighths over a sixteenth-note hi-hat pattern can really widen the groove. Have a listen.

DECORATIVE TOUCHES (USING ADDITIONAL TECHNIQUES TO ENHANCE YOUR BASS LINES)

Once you've gotten the hang of pluckin' and frettin', it's time to start trying some other techniques to give you more options and tonal variations. There are additional techniques for both hands, which we'll look at here.

Legato (Hammer-ons and Pull-offs)

Legato is yet another Italian musical term that basically means smooth and connected. It's the smoothest transition between two notes we can create on the bass. There are two techniques we use for this: *hammer-ons* (for ascending pitches) and *pull-offs* (for descending pitches).

Hammer-ons

Let's look at hammer-ons first. In the adjacent example, pluck the G note normally, fretting it with your first finger. For the following A note, sound the pitch by "hammering down" on the note with your third finger. The right hand is not used at all for this note. Notice the smooth, connected sound that results.

It will take a while to develop the finger strength needed for this move, but be patient. Soon it will feel as natural as eating with a fork. It's important to develop the ability to hammer on with any finger of the left hand. In the following examples, we'll use every combination of left-hand fingers.

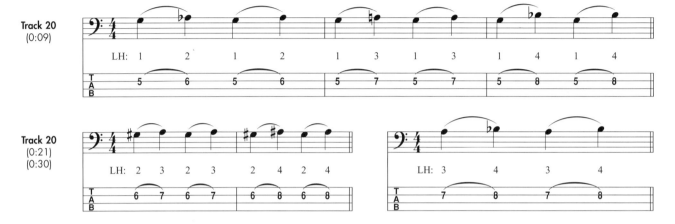

Track 20
(0:09)

Track 20
(0:21)
(0:30)

audio
tracks
21

Pull-offs

Pull-offs are essentially the opposite of hammer-ons. In the adjacent example, pluck the A note normally, fretting with your third finger. While you're fretting this note, you need to have the G note below it fretted with your first finger. The G is sounded by "pulling off" the string with your third finger. You're essentially using the third finger to pluck the string.

As with hammer-ons, you must be able to pull off with any finger. The examples below take you through every combination of left-hand fingers.

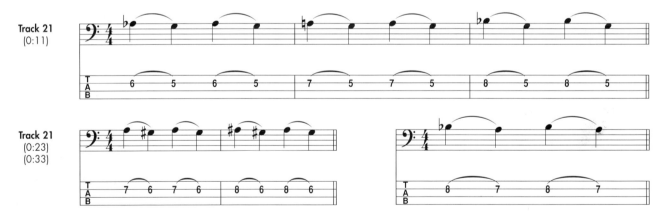

Track 21
(0:11)

Track 21
(0:23)
(0:33)

Slip-sliding Away

The musical term for a slide is *glissando*. While the human voice, a trombone, and a keyboard with a pitchwheel can create a true glissando, fretted instruments can only approximate. (Using a fretless bass is a different story, however. See Chapter 16.)

There are a few different ways slides are used. Let's take a look at the most common.

Ornamental

Sometimes a slide is used to simply get attention or to make one note stand out from the rest. These types of slides don't usually involve precise pitches. Rather, it's the effect that's wanted. You can think of these as sort of the bass version of the Jerry Lee Lewis–style glissando, in which you quickly drag your hand down the piano keyboard.

Note that sometimes the top note is not a specific pitch, while other times it is.

(0:00)
(0:06)

Scoops

Oftentimes, slides are used to scoop into notes, à la vocalists.

Track 22
(0:13)
(0:20)

Connecting Specific Pitches

Sometimes slides are used to simply connect two pitches that are played on the same string.

Track 23
(0:07)

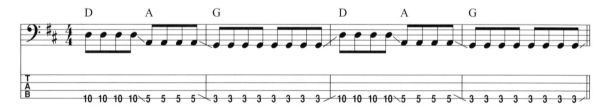

Legato (Slurred Gliss)

Finally, you can also use a slide in place of a hammer-on or a pull-off for a legato sound. In these examples, you pluck the first note, and then simply slide to the next note to sound it. This is a great technique to employ when you need to change positions.

(0:00)
(0:10)

Dead Notes (As Useful as Live Ones!)

A *dead note* is a percussive sound that can really help to make your bass lines shine. They're a subtle touch, but it's the type of thing you definitely miss when they're not around.

To play a dead note, lightly lay your hand across the strings so that your fingers are not touching the fretboard. Now pluck a string. You should hear a muted, percussive thud. Dead notes are often used in the middle of busy bass lines as sort of a rhythmic timekeeper. They can really inject some serious groove into your lines.

Let's take a look at some sample lines. Each line will be played twice—once without the dead notes and then with them.

Strange as it may seem, the grooves really come to life when the dead notes are brought in!

CHAPTER 10
MORE MUSICAL NOTATION LINGO & THEORY

What's Ahead:
- Additional music-notation terms
- Diatonic harmony
- Inversions
- The seven modes
- Additional scales

Just when you thought your head was about to explode from all the musical terms that have been crammed in there already, it's time to make room for some more. Now, now—it's not that bad, and you know it.

MORE NOTATIONAL SYMBOLS

Long ago, many people took the time to develop these conventions and symbols, so the least you can do is spend an hour or two and learn how they're used. Let's take a look at more symbols that you might come across.

Dynamics

There are numerous little dynamic markings that you may stumble upon. Though they are most common in classical music, they do make appearances in pop music, as well. Here are some of the most common:

- *mf (mezzo forte)*: Pronounced "met-so for-tay," this symbol means moderately loud. It's the average volume and what is implied when no dynamic marking is present.
- *f (forte)*: This means loud.
- *ff (fortissimo)*: Pronounced "for-tee-see-mo," this means very loud.
- *fff (fortississimo)*: This means very, very loud. (Now we're talking!)
- *mp (mezzo piano)*: This means moderately soft.
- *p (piano)*: This means soft.
- *pp (pianissimo)*: This means very soft.
- *ppp (pianississimo)*: This means very, very soft.

You get the idea. Basically, there are two ends of the spectrum: *piano* (soft) and *forte* (loud). If you add *mezzo* before either one of them, this indicates "moderately." Here, then, is the whole spectrum of dynamic markings in order of volume:

fff	*ff*	*f*	*mf*	*mp*	*p*	*pp*	*ppp*
(loudest)							(softest)

Theoretically, you could keep adding *f*'s or *p*'s in either direction, if needed. You might want to stop with the *f*'s once the cops show up, though.

Staccato

Another Italian word. Who did those guys think they were, anyway? Oh, well… To play a note *staccato* means to play it very short and abruptly. In other words, the note should not sustain at all. So if you're playing a fretted note, simply lift your finger off the fretboard immediately after playing the note. If you're playing an open string, you'll need to deaden the string immediately after with either your left or right hand.

Staccato is indicated by a dot placed over (or under) the notehead.

Grace Notes

A grace note is a quick ornamental note that precedes the main note. Grace notes can be higher or lower in pitch than their target pitch, although lower grace notes are much more common. They take up no real time in the music; basically, you cram them in at the last second, right before the target note. On the bass, we usually handle grace notes with hammer-ons, slides, or pull-offs (see Chapter 9).

(0:00) (0:09)
(0:17) (0:24)

Accent Marks

An accent mark looks like a greater-than symbol (>) and is placed next to the notehead either above or below the staff. When you see this symbol, you play this note slightly louder than the rest, thereby accenting it. This is a great way to breathe some life into your bass lines.

Repeat Sign

A repeat sign is a special type of bar line that tells the performer to play something that's written more than one time. There is usually an opening repeat sign and closing repeat sign. The measures surrounded by these signs are to be repeated before moving on.

Sometimes, the material inside the repeat signs is to be played more than twice. In those instances, specific directions are given at the closing repeat sign. In the following example, the material inside the repeat signs is to be played four times before moving on.

Track 29
(0:14)

Swung-eighths Notation

This symbol will sometimes appear at the top of the first page, next to the tempo. It tells the performer that the eighth notes are to be *swung* instead of played "straight." A swung eighth note is a lazy-sounding, lopsided eighth note that's very recognizable in jazz and blues styles. When you hear a "swing" or "shuffle" tune, the eighth notes are swung.

Technically, the eighth notes are the equivalent of the first and last notes of a triplet. Try counting "**1** & a, **2** & a, **3** & a, **4** & a." Swung eighth notes fall on the "**1**" and the "a" of each beat. It's somewhat difficult to grasp the concept on paper, but when you hear it, it's unmistakable.

Here's the same bass line played first as straight (normal) eighth notes, and then as swung eighths.

audio tracks 30

Track 30
(0:12)

Fermata

The *fermata* symbol tells the performer to break the tempo of the song and sustain a note for an indefinite amount of time. This is when the singer hits her final high note of the night and holds it out for 30 seconds before signaling the band back in.

If the fermata is held for a really long time, instrumentalists will sometimes repeatedly strike the note or chord for the duration. This is usually done with guitars, basses, or pianos, since we don't have a way of indefinitely sustaining a note. (Whereas violinists, for example, can keep bowing, and horn players or vocalists can sustain until their breath gives out.)

audio tracks 31

Ritard and A Tempo

A *ritard* is a gradual decrease in tempo that's often found at the end of a musical piece, when vocalists want to draw it out and savor every last moment they have on stage. OK, OK—it can be a nice effect as well, but that's another matter. A ritard is usually followed by a fermata (if it's at the end of the piece) or *a tempo*, which is a return to a normal tempo. If this tempo is different than what's marked at the beginning of the song, the new tempo will be given with the "a tempo" marking. Otherwise, you simply return to the original tempo.

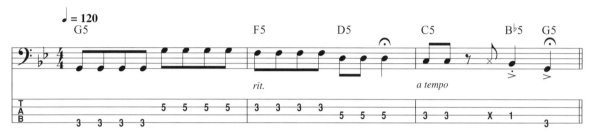

Crescendo and Decrescendo

A *crescendo* is a steady build in dynamics (volume), while a decrescendo is exactly the opposite. These devices are commonly used as an ensemble figure, meaning the entire band participates. Manipulating dynamics like this is a great way to really liven up an arrangement. While a crescendo is certainly more common, a cleverly placed *decrescendo* can be a real head-turner, as well.

Routing Directions

Before the days of copiers, computers, and notation programs, people actually had to write out every piece of music by hand. There was no copy-and-paste function. If you wanted an orchestra to play your piece, you had to write out the part for each player over and over again. Because of this, composers developed a way to minimize hand cramps; they used *routing directions*.

Simply put, these are musical symbols strategically placed throughout the score that essentially tell the performer things like, "go back to measure X, play through to measure Y, and then jump over to measure Z." A repeat sign is actually a very simplistic version of this system.

There are several different symbols used in routing directions:

- **D.C.** ("da capo"): This symbol tells the performer to return to the top ("head") of the musical piece and start again.
- **D.S.** ("dal segno"): This symbol tells the performer to return to the sign (𝄋) and start from there.
- **D.C. al Coda**: This tells the performer to return to the top, and then play until the "To Coda" symbol (⊕). The performer then jumps to the Coda section at the end.
- **D.S. al Coda**: This is the same as the previous instruction, but the performer starts at the sign instead of the top.

All of these signs are only acknowledged the first time you see them. In other words, after returning to the top from the D.C., you ignore it the next time you reach that spot and keep on moving through.

At first, this type of routing takes a bit of getting used to, but it sure saves a lot of paper!

DIATONIC HARMONY: THE FABRIC OF OUR LIVES

The word *diatonic* simply means "part of the key." For instance, in the key of C major, the notes C, D, E, F, G, A, and B are all diatonic. The other five notes (D♭, E♭, G♭, A♭, and B♭) are non-diatonic. So when we talk about diatonic harmony, we're talking about the chords and harmony that result from working with only the notes found in one particular key.

Harmonizing the Major Scale

We've already learned how to construct the different types of triads and seventh chords; now we're going to put them in context. We can build a triad (or seventh chord) off of every note in a major scale by simply stacking notes. Since a triad has three notes, we simply use one note as the root, skip a note, use the next note as the 3rd, skip a note, and then use the next note as the 5th. Let's take a look at this process in C major.

First, let's write out the C major scale with the degrees numbered.

Now, to build a triad off the first note (C), we simply use the aforementioned note-stacking method.

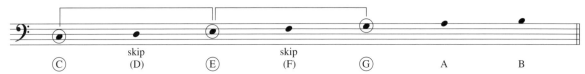

We end up with the notes C–E–G, which spells a C major triad. Let's build a triad off the second note in the scale (D), using the same stacking method.

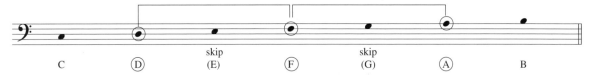

We end up with D–F–A, which spells a Dm triad. When we carry out this process for each note of the scale, we end up with seven triads:

C, Dm, Em, F, G, Am, B°

When a chord symbol appears by itself with no suffix, it implies a major triad.

When referring to the chords of a key, we use Roman numerals to identify them. Uppercase numerals are used for major chords, and lowercase numerals are used for minor and diminished chords. (The "o" symbol is additionally used with diminished chords.)

So here's what we've got so far:

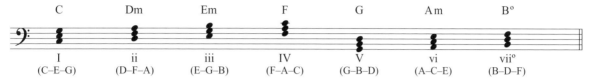

It turns out that this diatonic formula of chord qualities is true for any key. In other words, the diatonic ii chord will always be minor in every key. The diatonic IV chord will always be major in every key, etc.

Memorize this formula:

I   ii   iii   IV   V   vi   vii°

Using the Number System With Chord Progressions

Musicians will often use this Roman-numeral system instead of naming every chord in a progression. For instance, you might hear, "It's a I–IV–V in the key of C." This would mean the chords are I (C), IV (F), and V (G).

If you know your key signatures and, therefore, know your major scales, you simply locate the notes of the key's major scale and assign the appropriate chord qualities. For example, if you have a I–V–vi–IV in the key of D major, you would perform the following steps:

1. Write out the D major scale (consult the circle of 5ths): D–E–F♯–G–A–B–C♯.
2. Locate the first, fifth, sixth, and fourth notes of the scale: D, A, B, and G.
3. Determine the chord qualities for those scale degrees using the diatonic harmony formula: D (I), A (V), Bm (vi), and G (IV).

So your chord progression is D–A–Bm–G.

INVERSIONS

We've learned that a triad consists of three notes (root, 3rd, and 5th) and a seventh chord consists of four notes (root, 3rd, 5th, and 7th). However, those notes do not always need to appear in that order (from the root up). Many times chords appear in *inversion*.

Root Position

When a chord has its root as the lowest note, it is said to be in *root position*. This is what's implied when you simply see a chord symbol.

First Inversion

If we were to transfer the lowest note (the root) up an octave, we'd be left with the 3rd on the bottom. This is *first inversion*. The chord symbol will reflect this by using a slash. The name to the left will be the chord, and on the right will be the bass note.

Second Inversion

If we continue this process and again move the lowest note (now the 3rd) up an octave, we're left with the 5th on the bottom. This is *second inversion*. Again, the chord symbol represents this change with a slash.

If we were to continue this process once more, we'd end up in root position again, with the root on the bottom. So a triad can only appear in root position, first inversion, or second inversion.

However, a seventh chord has four notes, so it can appear in *third inversion*, as well. See below.

Here's how these shapes look on the bass as arpeggios:

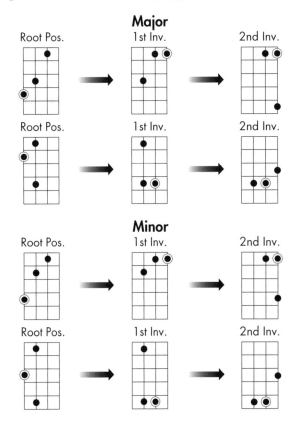

You can really flex your bass muscles with inversions, as they can give a chord progression a different color. Check out the following examples:

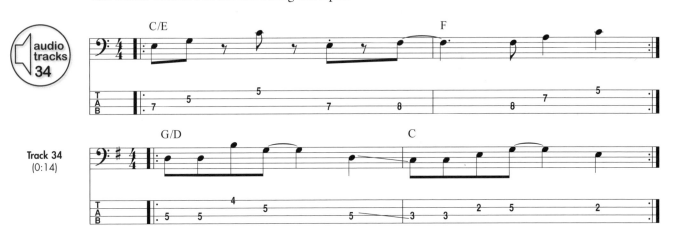

MODES: JUST WHEN YOU THOUGHT IT WAS SAFE TO PLAY A MAJOR SCALE

OK, so you know your major scales, right? Are you satisfied yet? "Scales are so much fun," you say. "I want to learn more!" Well, you're in luck! We still have to learn about *modes*, and there are seven of them. (Technically, you'll only have to learn five, because you already know two of them—you just don't know it yet!) Here are the names of the seven modes (and more strange words for you to memorize):

Ionian   Dorian   Phrygian   Lydian   Mixolydian   Aeolian   Locrian

There are two ways to look at modes. One way is to treat each one as its own scale with its own formula. The other way is to think of them as seven different names for a major scale. We'll start with the second method.

But I Thought I Already Knew a Major Scale?

Well, you may know a major scale, but do you really know it inside and out? The seven modes are basically seven scales that start and end on each note of a major scale. Confused? Don't worry—it's not that complicated.

Let's take a G major scale. The key signature for G major is… anyone?… anyone? That's right—one sharp, F♯. So a G major scale is spelled: G–A–B–C–D–E–F♯. Congratulations, you know your first mode. The first mode is called *Ionian*, and it's the same exact thing as a major scale. So G Ionian is the same thing as the G major scale.

Now, for the second mode (*Dorian*), we simply start on the second note of the G major scale and build a scale from there, using the key signature of G major.

A Dorian

You end up with the notes A–B–C–D–E–F♯–G. This is A Dorian, the second mode of G major. We can continue this process with each note of the G major scale, and when we're done, we'll have seven modes.

Here's what we'll end up with:

I mentioned that you already knew two of these modes. G Ionian, as we said, is the same as G major. And E Aeolian is the same as the E minor scale (the relative minor of G major). So Ionian and Aeolian are just alternative names for the major scale and the minor scale, respectively.

Modes are Scales, Too!

While it's easiest to grasp the concept of modes by using the major-scale reference, it's also important to be able to relate to each one as its own scale and learn its scale formula. We do this by comparing them to the major or minor scale. If a mode contains a major 3rd, we say it's a major mode. If it contains a minor 3rd, we say it's a minor mode. Let's go through the following modes, which are all built from a C root, and analyze them, one by one.

Ionian

C Ionian

Obviously, this is a major mode. It's the same as the major scale.

     Formula: 1–2–3–4–5–6–7

     C Ionian: C–D–E–F–G–A–B

Dorian

C Dorian

Dorian is a minor mode because it contains a minor 3rd. It's thought of as a minor scale with a raised 6th tone.

     Formula: 1–2–♭3–4–5–6–♭7

     C Dorian: C–D–E♭–F–G–A–B♭

Phrygian

C Phrygian

Phrygian is another minor mode. It's similar to the minor scale, but with a ♭2nd.

     Formula: 1–♭2–♭3–4–5–♭6–♭7

     C Phrygian: C–D♭–E♭–F–G–A♭–B♭

Lydian

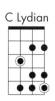

C Lydian

Lydian is a major mode, and a very bright-sounding one at that. It's similar to the major scale, but with a raised 4th tone.

     Formula: 1–2–3–♯4–5–6–7

     C Lydian: C–D–E–F♯–G–A–B

Mixolydian

C Mixolydian

Mixolydian is another major mode and further qualified as a *dominant* mode because of its ♭7th degree.

     Formula: 1–2–3–4–5–6–♭7

     C Mixolydian: C–D–E–F–G–A–B♭

Aeolian

C Aeolian

Aeolian is another name for the minor scale, so it's obviously a minor mode.

     Formula: 1–2–♭3–4–5–♭6–♭7

     C Aeolian: C–D–E♭–F–G–A♭–B♭

Locrian

Locrian is a minor mode and further qualified as a *diminished* mode because of its unstable ♭5th degree. It's similar to the minor scale, but with a ♭2nd and a ♭5th.

　　　Formula: 1–♭2–♭3–4–♭5–♭6–♭7
　　　C Locrian: C–D♭–E♭–F–G♭–A♭–B♭

C Locrian

Origin of Modes

The origin of the modes can be traced all the way back to the sixth century and beyond. The actual names of the modes come from references to ancient Greek cities that were said to prefer the sound of their namesake modes. (All of those names weren't exactly the same as the ones we have today, but several of them were.)

　　　In the ninth century, the church of medieval Europe misinterpreted a text written in the sixth century in which certain Greek musical theories had been translated into Latin. Therefore, the church modes (which are the direct ancestors of the modes we use today) began to be referred to by the Greek names to which they were not related—musically speaking, that is.

　　　By the sixteenth century, a Swiss theorist named Henricus Glareanus published Dodekachordon, and the concept of the church modes was firmly set into place. Throughout the years, after being exposed to the then undiscovered conventions of the Western tonal harmony we use today, these modes have been altered into the modern-day versions.

By far, the most common modes are Ionian, Dorian, Mixolydian, and Aeolian. Lydian and Phrygian see occasional use (Lydian is more common in jazz), and Locrian is rarely used. Let's take a look at some grooves in these common modes to help get their sound into your ears.

(0:00)
(0:18)

(0:00)
(0:13)

OTHER "NOTABLE" SCALES

There are still a few other important scales we've yet to cover, so free up some brain cells and listen up. Don't have any left? Well, if you still remember your locker combination from the sixth grade, those brain cells will do nicely. And how many lines from that "I'm Too Sexy" song can you still recite? I rest my case.

Major Pentatonic

The *major pentatonic* scale is a cheery five-note ("penta") scale that's created from omitting the 4th and 7th tones of the major scale. Consequently, those tones create the most musical tension in the major scale. By eliminating those notes, we have, in the major pentatonic, perhaps the most failsafe scale of all. Soloists often rely on pentatonic scales when improvising because of this: there aren't any "iffy" notes.

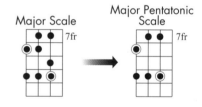

Formula: 1–2–3–5–6
C major pentatonic: C–D–E–G–A

You'll hear this scale in plenty of bass lines, especially in Motown-style R&B. Here it is in action:

(0:00)
(0:17)

Minor Pentatonic

Equally popular is the *minor pentatonic* scale, which is created by omitting the 2nd and ♭6th tones of the minor scale. This one is a real riff-meister; it's used extensively in blues, classic rock, country, funk, and more.

Formula: 1–♭3–4–5–♭7
C minor pentatonic: C–E♭–F–G–B♭

Let's check it out:

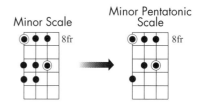

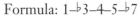

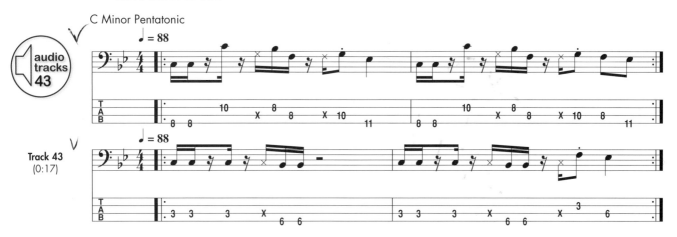

Track 43
(0:17)

Blues Scale

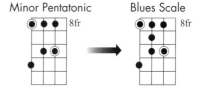

The *blues scale* and the minor pentatonic are partners in crime. The blues scale is actually a minor pentatonic with one added note: the ♭5th. This one's used a great deal in… well, blues. But it's also shown some love in hard rock, classic rock, and country lead guitar.

Formula: 1–♭3–4–♭5–5–♭7
C blues scale: C–E♭–F–G♭–G–B♭

Harmonic Minor

The *harmonic minor* scale is a wicked little ditty that's very popular in classical music; however, it doesn't get much airtime in popular genres these days. Basically, it's the minor scale with a raised 7th tone. This creates the awkward interval of an augmented 2nd (3 half steps) between the ♭6th and the 7th degrees.

Formula: 1–2–♭3–4–5–♭6–7
C harmonic minor: C–D–E♭–F–G–A♭–B

Melodic Minor

The *melodic minor* scale was created after the harmonic minor to help ease the awkwardness of the augmented 2nd interval. It's the minor scale with a raised 6th and 7th tone. It's a very unique scale, because the bottom half sounds like a minor scale, while the top half sounds like a major scale. Outside of jazz and classical music, where it's used quite extensively, this scale doesn't see much action.

Formula: 1–2–♭3–4–5–6–7
C melodic minor: C–D–E♭–F–G–A–B

Chromatic

The *chromatic* scale simply contains all 12 notes. Start at one note, play every single note between it and its octave, and you've got the chromatic scale. This scale is rarely used in its entirety. Rather, soloists occasionally make use of chromatic notes to color phrases.

Chromatic Scale

Formula: 1–♭2–2–♭3–3–4–♭5–5–♭6–6–♭7–7
C chromatic: C–D♭–D–E♭–E–F–G♭–G–A♭–A–B♭–B

Now listen to how bits of this scale can be used to spice up a bass line.

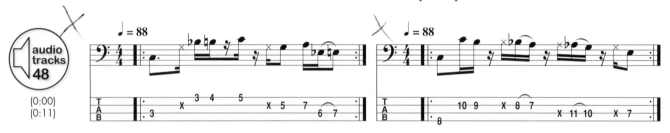

(0:00)
(0:11)

All right, that's it! You're in the clear now—no more new scales, chords, or music symbols to learn.*

*Topics covered subject to change without notice. Price does not include tax, title, and license.

Answers to Chord-Progression Test:
(You'd better not be peeking before you take the test!)

1. D–G–A	6. B♭–F–Gm–Am
2. D–A	7. E♭–Cm–A♭–B♭
3. Am–D	8. E–A–E–C♯m
4. Dm–E♭–F	9. F♯–E–B
5. C–Am–F	10. A♭–Fm–B♭m–Cm

CHAPTER 11

SEIZING THE MOMENT: PLAYING FILLS AND SOLOS

What's Ahead:

- Scaling the second octave: two-octave scale and arpeggio shapes
- Filling in the gaps—bass-style
- Getting your "lead bass" feet wet with melodies and solos

OK, so I know all we've been talking about up to this point has been how bassists play a supporting role, and this and that. However, opportunities do arise once in a while when the bassist gets his day in the sun. Whether it's a brief one-measure fill or—gasp!—an actual solo, we need to be prepared to step up to the plate and swing away.

HIGHER AND HIGHER: MAKING YOUR WAY INTO THE NEXT OCTAVE

One of the reasons that vocals, guitars, saxophones, and the like are often featured as soloists is because their range is ideal. Humans hear in the lower midrange of the sound spectrum, more or less, and those instruments fill that register nicely. So, when it's time for us to solo, we need to do our best to get up there and be heard. This is where the higher octaves come into play. (However, if you're soloing to an audience full of whales, feel free to stay as low as possible.)

Left-hand fingering is crucial in these scale shapes, as it facilitates the shifting process. Therefore, try out the left hand. fingerings provided for these shapes, as they'll help make the transitions smooth.

Two-Octave Scale Shapes

Let's find out how to turn the scale shapes we already know into two-octave shapes. This will require a shift in position, which will take a bit of getting used to. Just remember to take your time in the beginning; the speed will come with steady repetition.

Major Scale    Minor Scale 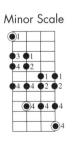   Major Pentatonic 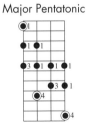   Minor Pentatonic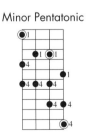

Two-Octave Arpeggio Shapes

Triads

Major	Minor	Augmented	Diminished
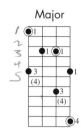		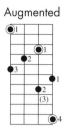	

7th Chords

Major 7	Minor 7	Dominant 7	Minor 7♭5	Diminished 7
				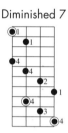

Learning the Entire Fretboard: The 2-and-2 Rule

It's common for beginners to learn the lower portion of the fretboard first, and this makes sense. However, the upper range of your instrument need not remain an enigma. There's an easy trick that will help you decode the notes of the entire fretboard. I call it the "2-and-2 rule," which is short for "2 frets higher, 2 strings higher."

The first thing you need to do is memorize the notes on the low E and A strings. This won't take as long as you think, since most of the bass lines we play are rooted on one of these strings. Study the fretboard chart on the reference page at the end of this book until you have these strings memorized. (And be sure to notice, if you hadn't already, that the notes start all over again after the twelfth fret.)

To learn the notes on the other two strings (D and G), use the 2-and-2 rule. If you move two frets higher and two strings higher from any note on the E string, you'll end up with the same note, an octave higher, on the D string. If you start on an A string note and move two frets up and two strings up, you'll end up with the same note, an octave higher, on the G string. Check it out.

So you can use this method to transpose whole phrases up an octave, which is a nice effect in and of itself.

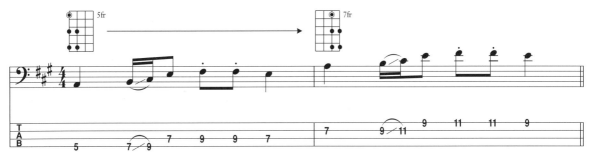

Any time you have a phrase that takes place on only the bottom two strings, use the 2-and-2 rule to transpose it up an octave. This will help you learn the fretboard faster.

FILLING THE GAPS

A *fill* is a brief phrase (usually one measure long or less) that helps to maintain interest during a musical transition or "dead spot." Typical places you might find fills include between vocal phrases, at the end of a section (verse, chorus, etc.), and during an extended one-chord section, among others. All instruments play fills at one time or another: guitars, keys, drums, and, yes, bass!

When constructing a fill, there are a few things you need to know in order to pull it off smoothly:

- **The key of the song**: This will let you know which melodic material (scales, arpeggios, etc.) will be usable during the fill.

- **Where you're ending up**: You need to have a clear idea of where you are in the measure and where you're headed so you can land on your feet.

- **What else is going on**: Is the guitar player taking a fill here, as well? What about the drums? If too many people join in, it will start to sound a bit like a train wreck. Learn to be cognizant of what the other members in the band are doing.

- **The fill's length**: Do you have two beats or two measures? You don't want to dive into a really complicated line if you don't have time to wrap it up.

What Do I Play?

OK, so you're ready to strut your stuff, but with what? Let's look at some commonly used material for fill-building.

Major Pentatonic Scale

Pentatonics are probably the most commonly used scales during fills because they're so "safe." It's hard to hit a really sour-sounding note. The major pentatonic works beautifully in major keys; simply use the scale with the same root as the key you're playing in. For example, if you're in the key of G, use the G major pentatonic.

Minor Pentatonic Scale

The minor pentatonic works perfectly in minor keys, but it's also used quite a bit in bluesy major-key tunes. Whereas the major pentatonic will sound prettier, the minor pentatonic will sound tougher and bluesier.

Major and Minor Scales

Use these over their corresponding key. These provide you with two more note choices than the pentatonics. This means more color, but it also means a greater chance of playing something that sounds a little odd. You should think these through before wingin' it on the gig.

Arpeggios

Arpeggios are fair game, as well. However, they tend to sound a little lame and predictable if you just run up and down them in straight eighth or sixteenth notes. Mix the notes up, repeat certain notes, etc.

The aforementioned advice regarding mixing it up and not playing straight up and down arpeggios applies to scales, as well. We initially learn them that way so we can get the sound in our ears and the notes under our fingers. However, when it's time to draw from them in a real musical environment, we usually don't play them straight through.

Other Concepts

The notes you choose make up only half the fill. Remember, there are many other ways to get the most out of those notes: rests, imitative phrasing, syncopation, octave transference, sequences, varied articulation (staccato and legato), varied dynamics, etc. The possibilities are truly limitless.

With that in mind, let's take a look at some examples.

Getting Down to It: Fills in Action

This first example is a fairly typical situation. The end of a chorus will sometimes contain an extended I chord, allowing the energy to come back down before the next verse. If the guitar player is sustaining a chord, which is fairly common, this is a great opportunity for you to steal some limelight. Here are four different takes on the same situation. They're all one-measure fills in the key of G.

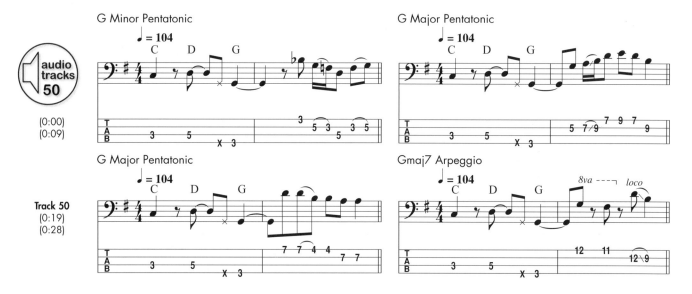

You can also use brief fills to maintain interest within a section. For instance, you may play the same groove for three measures during a verse and then throw in a short fill during the fourth measure to coincide with the ending of a phrase. Let's take a look at how that sounds.

The first two examples show a funky groove based around a C7 tonality. Example 1 uses the C blues scale with one chromatic passing tone (B♮), while example 2 uses a sequence based on a C7 arpeggio. The last two examples demonstrate a more diatonic pop-rock groove in C. Example 3 uses the C major pentatonic, while example 4 makes use of an Fmaj7 arpeggio for a bright-sounding fill.

Although fills usually occur at the end of a phrase, there's no steadfast rule that says they can't occur in other places, as well. Try plugging in one during the middle of a phrase (during practice—not during the gig!) sometimes to keep it interesting. If it doesn't work, it doesn't work. But you may end up with something really memorable.

STICKING YOUR NECK OUT THERE: PLAYING SOLOS AND MELODIES

On rare occasions (although not that rare in jazz), we bassists actually get to ride high above the sonic waves with melodies and solos. Although this is no cause for alarm, it can, at times, be a little like a fish being out of water. Because we spend so much time developing our craft as a supportive instrument, the idea of playing lead doesn't come very naturally. The following will help prepare you for your time in the spotlight.

Bringing the Bass into the Spotlight

Though the bass was once thought of as firmly seated in the background of music, this is not the case today. Several important players have contributed to the bass's liberation from this role, including John Entwistle (The Who), Paul McCartney (The Beatles), and perhaps most of all, James Jamerson, the legendary Motown bassist who played on more hits than the Beatles, Elvis, and the Beach Boys combined.

In realms outside of pop music, Jaco Pastorius and Stanley Clarke moved the bass to the forefront with their horn-like solos and unprecedented virtuosity. Since then, the bass has been accepted and celebrated as an instrument capable of any musical function.

©Tom Copi/MICHAEL OCHS ARCHIVES.COM
Jaco Pastorius

Photo by Ken Settle
John Entwistle

©MICHAEL OCHS ARCHIVES.COM
James Jamerson

Photo by Ken Settle
Paul McCartney

Tackling the Melody on Bass

Melody isn't an entirely new concept. We play melodic bass lines all the time. However, outside of jazz or fusion, the bass rarely states the main melody. Melodic instruments usually take certain liberties with melodies to help them sound a little livelier. This is especially true with rather basic melodies.

To help demonstrate this, we'll take a simple melody and work through it several times, adding more inflections and taking more liberties with each pass.

We'll start with a basic melody.

The first thing we need to do is move it to the next octave so we can be more easily heard.

This is a fairly basic melody, with no syncopation and few long notes. While singers and horn players can shape these melodies somewhat with their use of dynamics (they can swell in and out of notes), vibrato, and timbre, we bassists are a bit more limited. However, we can make the melody more personal in other ways. Sure, we can employ dynamics to a degree, but there are other ways to skin a cat. For instance, we can slightly alter the rhythm to add some syncopation.

In this variation, we anticipate the half notes of measures 2, 3, and 4 by an eighth note.

The next variation presents more rhythmic possibilities and also introduces some slurred glisses. Pay attention to the tab here because we're changing position a few times to facilitate the slides. Notice that the melody is starting to take on more of a vocal-like character.

Finally, in the last one we've added some grace-note slides and a few melodic *turns* (pull-off/ hammer-on combinations) in measures 3 and 4. Grace notes are an excellent way to lend a vocal quality to a melody. Singers scoop into notes all the time, and grace notes are our closest approximation to these scoops.

Now, take a look back at the original melody and see how far we've come. While the original contour of the melody is still intact, we've added some life to it with an interpretation that's all our own.

How do you make your melody lines more vocal-like? Try singing along with what you're playing! It may sound obvious, but it's a great tool in more ways than one. It will help to train your ear, but it will also remind us to use rests, grace notes, dynamics, and more when we play our melodies because these types of embellishments are much more apparent when we sing.

Solo Time

Melodies are one thing, but solos are something quite different. When you're playing a melody, you're usually interpreting something that's pre-composed. With solos, however, you could be *improvising*—making it up on the fly! While the subject of improvising is too massive to cover in detail here, there are a few key things to consider. Since this is new ground for us in more ways than one, let's start by pointing out some things that will help us make the most of our time in the limelight.

- **The rhythm section is doing their job**: When you're the soloist, you don't need to be worrying about maintaining the groove; that's the job of the rhythm section. And when you're soloing, it's your one chance to shed those rhythm section duties. Take this opportunity to stretch out, rhythmically speaking. It's really quite fun to rub across and blur the beat, and make a strong musical statement, as well. Just listen to blues solos for an example of this.

- **Make the most of your instrument's range**: As bassists, we spend most of our time in the bottom half of our range. However, soloing is a different animal and requires us to put those high little frets to use. (We paid for them, so we may as well use them!)

- **Pull out those effects**: When you're soloing, you're not responsible for being the foundation. All ears (well, a lot of ears) are on you. So if you've been looking for the opportunity to try out that distortion or delay pedal, this is as good of a time as any. See Chapter 22 to get an idea of the available effects.

- **Interact with the rhythm section**: Just because you're temporarily not part of the rhythm-section team doesn't mean you sever all relations with them. Make eye contact and get them to respond to your soloing. If you're really hammering away on a rhythmic idea and want the rest of the band to accent it with you, do your best to convey that with eye signals and body movements. Or give them the signal to drop it down to a whisper and make a dramatic statement. The more you play with certain band members, the easier this type of communication becomes, and it can really inject a new life into your solos.

Let's take a look at a few lead phrases to get our feet wet. While many different scales are used when improvising, the minor pentatonic is arguably the most common. Here, we'll work out of A minor pentatonic.

In the first example, we've got some slides combined with some syncopation for a catchy phrase that's got plenty of attitude. The second example adds the ♭5th (E♭) from the A blues scale and finishes off with some grace-note hammer-ons. Try playing these same phrases without the slides and grace notes to hear the difference. You'll realize why these devices are so important.

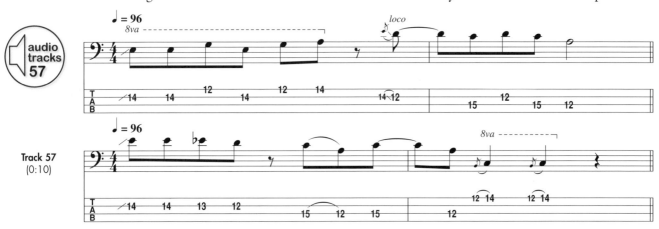

audio tracks 57

Track 57 (0:10)

Solos are also a great place to showoff. *Sequences* are often used to create speedy licks to impress the audience. Here are a few examples using the A minor pentatonic scale in twelfth position. The first descends through the scale in a triplet-based sequence, while the second is essentially the opposite. The final two examples show a similar approach with sixteenth notes. A distortion pedal is kicked on during the latter two examples for fun.

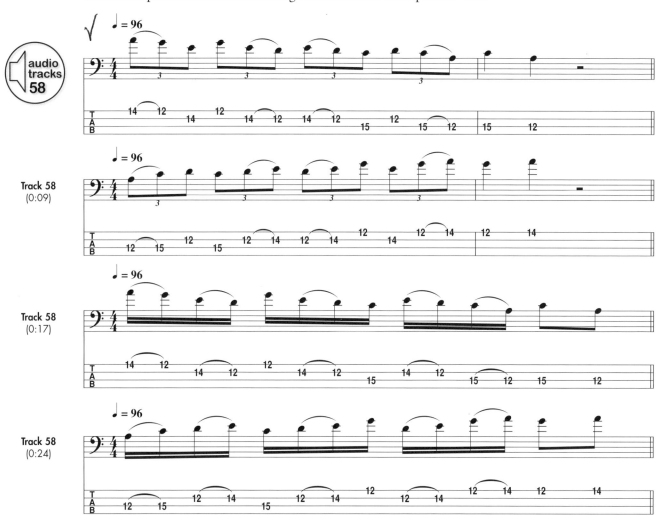

TRANSCRIBING AND PLAYING BY EAR

No, I don't mean using your ear to pluck the strings on your bass. (Although, now that you mention it, it could be a cool gimmick, I suppose.) Playing by ear simply means being able to play without the aid of sheet music. It's the ability to recognize something you hear and reproduce it on your instrument. *Transcribing* is one of the best ways to get to this point. Transcribing is the act of sitting down and figuring out something from a song and writing it down. This can be bass lines, melodies, chords, etc.

Simply put, music is a language. We learn language as a young child by imitation and repetition—we don't even think about it. Music is the same way. The more you're exposed to it, the more you'll recognize the familiar patterns used and be able to recreate them yourself. There are certain chord progressions (I–IV–V, for example) or licks that you've probably heard thousands of times throughout your life. When you begin to study these things by transcribing them from records, you begin the assimilation process. You start to recognize them without having to grab your bass.

To get started, take a favorite bass line of yours and try to figure it out. I'd recommend writing it down in musical notation as well, because this will train not only your ear but also your music-reading skills. Here are some things to remember when you start transcribing:

- **Be patient**: You didn't learn to speak (or read) English in one day; it took years. Don't expect to "speak" music in one week; it takes time.

- **Get in tune**: Most albums are in tune with A440 (universal tuning note whose frequency is 440 vibrations per second). It will be much easier to figure out the bass lines if you're in tune.

- **Work on small phrases**: Listen to the whole song a few times through, but when you're ready to start transcribing, work on one or two measures at a time. The more proficient you become, the more you'll be able to digest longer sections at once.

- **Take breaks**: Your ear can become fatigued with repeated listening. It's important that you get refreshed every once in a while. Work for an hour or 45 minutes and then take a 15-minute walk. You'll be much more productive this way.

- **Get a half-speed device**: There are many devices on the market that allow you to slow the audio down without changing the pitch. Both software and hardware versions are available. If you're working on a line that's too quick for you to figure out, a half-speed device will do wonders.

Once you've gotten comfortable transcribing some bass lines, try some other instruments. Transcribing is a skill that takes practice, but the rewards are well worth it. You'll develop your ear tremendously, as well as your musical memory. Eventually, with enough practice, you'll be able to hear most songs once or twice and know the chord progression without having to even pick up your bass.

Styles

CHAPTER 12
ROCKIN', ROLLIN', AND TWO-STEPPIN': ROCK AND COUNTRY STYLES

> ***What's Ahead:***
> - The foundation of rock styles
> - Early rock 'n' roll
> - Hard rock
> - Pop rock
> - Country

Rock 'n' roll. Who knew 50 years ago what it would become today? Lucky for us, it survived the disapproval of countless disgruntled parents throughout its infancy and has blossomed into one of the broadest styles in pop-music history. There's pop rock, hard rock, country rock, blues rock, jazz rock, folk rock, prog rock, neo-classical rock… You can just about put any musical style in front of "rock" and have another subgenre. (And if you can imagine it, rest assured that people have probably tried it!) However, all of these subgenres are bound by some common threads that lie at the heart of the rock style. Rock has a certain energy, drive, and beat that's unmistakable.

THE FOUNDATIONS OF ROCK 'N' ROLL

Rock music draws from many other genres and makes their elements its own. However, there are a few traits within the rock style that lie at the heart of its appeal.

The Backbeat: Where Rock 'n' Roll Gets Its Heart and Soul

It's really hard to believe that before rock 'n' roll came along, the drum set as we know it wasn't a staple of pop music. The electric bass as we know it also didn't exist, and therefore, the instrument (upright bass, that is) was usually relegated to the "felt, not heard" status on most recordings. Now, over 50 years later, it's almost impossible to imagine popular music without them. Rock's appeal infected virtually all popular music in its path, and its core elements crept their way into other styles, far and wide.

Perhaps one of the most crucial of those elements is the *backbeat*. The backbeat is what you clap along with: beats 2 and 4. At least, it's what you're supposed to clap on! There are always those few rhythmically challenged people in the crowd clapping at the opposite time of everyone else. Those people are clapping on beats 1 and 3, and we don't associate with them!

Attitude to Spare

Rock music is all about attitude. You don't just play rock; you feel it! Conviction goes a long way in the business of rock, and that's something to always keep in mind. Rock music, similarly to blues, breaks all kinds of music-theory "rules." The only thing that makes it work is the fact that the performers mean to break those rules, and they look cool while doing it!

Let's take a look at how all of this relates to bass lines in the rock style. Keep these concepts in mind when working through the following examples. It will help lend authenticity to the style.

EIGHTH NOTES REVISITED: THE CORNERSTONE OF EARLY ROCK

When it comes to rock's early days, nothing got the job done on the bass more than eighth notes. Whether it's plugging away on root notes or weaving up and down through arpeggios, eighth notes were the bassist's best friend. Since we've spent some time with eighths earlier, in Chapter 8, we'll look at how we can dress up the approach with some of the various techniques we've covered thus far.

We'll start with the basic eighth-note line:

Now, there's nothing wrong with this approach, and it has certainly fit the bill many times. But now let's take a look at some of the many possibilities that exist for varying this line while still keeping with the eighth-note approach.

You can see that varying even one note can add a whole new dimension to the line. The use of slides, chromatic passing/approach tones, and arpeggios can result in an almost limitless amount of variations.

HARD ROCK: RIFFING AND NAILING THE ROOTS

In the realm of hard rock, two main elements prevail: *nailing the roots* and *riffs*. Let's sink our teeth into each. It should also be mentioned that the pick is much more common in this style than in others. This is due to the fact that the pick can get a more biting attack than the fingers, which often suits this music well.

Nailing the Roots: A Rhythmic Workout

In harder rock styles, the note choice is often simplified in favor of more complex rhythms. Though eighth notes certainly have their say, sixteenth notes play an increased role, as well. Let's take a look at a typical minor hard-rock progression (A5–G5) and the different rhythmic approaches we might take while sticking to the roots.

When using sixteenth notes, it's common to pick all downstrokes for the eighth notes and bring *alternate picking* (picking with alternating up and downstrokes) into play for the sixteenths. Pay attention to the picking directions in the following examples: (⊓) = down-stroke, (V) = upstroke.

You can get a lot of mileage out of two root notes simply by adjusting the rhythms slightly. With the use of rests, as in the last example, dynamic effects can be achieved.

Adding Syncopation in the Sixteenth-note Realm

When you add some syncopation to sixteenth notes, you enter a new dimension of rhythmic possibilities. However, when using a pick, this presents new technical challenges. To keep from getting your pick hand all confused, we make use of *ghost strokes*, or the purposeful "missing" of the string during a stroke. This allows you to keep your right hand steadily moving with the beat and takes the guess work out of the direction of the pick strokes. Here's how it works.

Let's say you start with this rhythm:

Notice that you're always playing downstrokes on the eighth notes. The only time the upstroke comes into play is the last sixteenth note of each beat (i.e., the "a" of each beat: 1 (e) & **a**, 2 (e) & **a**, etc.). You may not realize it, but you're already making use of ghost strokes. You pick down on beat 1, and then bring your pick back up on the "e" of the beat without picking the string. Then you pick down on the "&" of the beat before picking up on the "a" of the beat. That action, of bringing your pick back up without making contact with the string after your first downstroke, is essentially a ghost stroke.

In other words, you could think of the first rhythm as straight sixteenth notes, but you're purposefully missing the second note in each beat.

It's this concept—keeping your right hand moving but strategically missing certain notes—that defines the use of ghost strokes.

Now let's look at some more complex rhythms for our A5–G5 chord progression, paying special attention to the picking directions. The ghost strokes appear in parentheses.

Track 62
(0:15)

*The *sim.* annotation stands for "simile," which means to continue a certain pattern in the same vein. In this instance, it applies to the picking pattern from measure 1.

Hard Rock Riffs

A *riff* is a short musical phrase that doesn't necessarily suggest a specific harmony. Much hard rock is riff-based rather than chord-based. The most common scales used for riffing in hard rock are the minor pentatonic scale and the blues scale.

The blues scale is the same as the minor pentatonic scale, only it has one extra note: the ♭5th.

There are several elements at work in these types of riffs:

- **Imitation**: Note how the second example makes use of this device to lend continuity throughout.

- **Syncopation**: Syncopation is indispensable for injecting energy and life into a riff. Steady eighth notes can have their place, but an offbeat accent every now and then can really maintain the listener's interest.

- **Sequence**: A musical *sequence* is a repetition of a musical phrase or idea at a different pitch level. Notice how, in the last example, the E–E♭ motive is followed by an E♭–D motive. Sequences, when used in short doses as to not be too obvious and, therefore, predictable, can also lend familiarity and cohesiveness to a phrase.

The "N.C." you sometimes see in place of a chord symbol stands for "no chord." It's common to see this when you have a riff that doesn't necessarily suggest a chord tonality.

Occasionally, other chromatic notes are used to create an even more menacing sound. The ♭2nd scale degree (B♭ in the key of A) is a popular choice in this regard.

POP ROCK: THE SONG COMES FIRST

The pop-rock subgenre is so expansive that it had to be included. Yet, it's so expansive that it's somewhat difficult to distill down to its core elements. Under the massive stylistic umbrella of "pop rock," you'll find countless other subgenres, including, at one time or another, country rock, folk rock, singer/songwriter, blues rock, alternative rock, emo, and punk rock, among others. However, the common thread that binds all of these styles is the simple fact that the song comes first; it's usually your job to play what the song needs and nothing more.

The Vocals Rule

In almost all pop rock, the vocals are *the* most important part. Therefore, it's of utmost importance that you don't step on them. This usually means keeping it fairly simple and straightforward. This doesn't mean that you can't have any fun, but you must keep in mind that you're doing your job best when you help the vocals shine.

Let's look at a few typical approaches to some common pop-rock progressions.

Notice that none of these lines are fancy, but some of them do make use of little devices to add interest to the line. The second example uses dead notes, while the next makes use of staccato to add punch; the last adds a few approach tones to an otherwise straight eighth-note line. They're staying out of the way of the vocal but still adding something to the mix. Subtlety is the name of the game here.

LEARN FROM THE PROS!

Here we'll see these concepts put to use in some rock classics. From the riffs of "Come Together" and "Would?" to the supportive roles in "Synchronicity II" and "Beast of Burden," you get to see how the pros make these concepts work for them.

All Shook Up

Words and Music by
Otis Blackwell and Elvis Presley

Come Together

Words and Music by
John Lennon and Paul McCartney

Money

Words and Music by
Roger Waters

Synchronicity II

Music and Lyrics by Sting

Beast of Burden

Would?

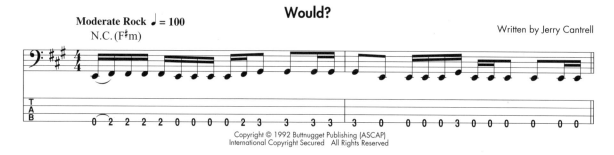

BOTH STYLES OF MUSIC: COUNTRY & WESTERN

As the years pass, the lines between country and rock (pop rock, at least) continue to blur more and more. Certainly, with the rise of "young country" mega-stars Garth Brooks, Tim McGraw, Shania Twain, and the like, the larger-than-life stadium concert antics that were once lodged firmly in the rock idiom are now equally enjoyed by country performers. But it's not just the concerts that have grown similar. Country music's instrumentation has firmly crossed over into the pop realm, and the backing bands of the genre possess some of the finest musicians around.

Roots and 5ths

If there's any one sound that's identifiable as country bass, it's the root/5th approach. Whether it's a fast, knee-slapping hoedown or a slow, graceful country waltz, you simply can't go wrong with this approach.

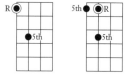

The basic concept involves playing the root on the downbeat followed by the 5th of the chord (either above or below the root).

Here we see the pattern applied to a lazy country shuffle.

Here's what it sounds like on an up-tempo country two-beat. The first example sticks to nothing but roots and 5ths, but the second example shows how walking up to the next root can add interest, as well. Depending on where your next root is located, you may have to get a little creative. The C walks nicely up to F by way of the C major scale in measure 2, but we have to add a lower tone and a chromatic tone in measure 4 when walking up from F to G.

During a slow waltz, you can stick to roots and 5ths, as well. You can also make use of connecting tones, as in the following example.

When it comes to pop country or country rock, you can usually approach either music form with the same mentality as pop rock. Always remember that the vocals are the focus, and your role is subservient to them. You help to make them sound good.

LEARN FROM THE PROS!

Let's take a look at some bass lines from a few country classics.

Hello Mary Lou

Words and Music by
Gene Pitney and C. Mangiaracina

Your Cheatin' Heart

Words and Music by
Hank Williams

Alcohol

Words and Music by
Brad Paisley

Friends in Low Places

Words and Music by DeWayne Blackwell
and Earl Bud Lee

Crazy

Words and Music by
Willie Nelson

CHAPTER 13
THE BLUES AND ALL THAT JAZZ

What's Ahead:
- The 12-bar blues form
- Arpeggio-based blues shuffle lines
- Slow blues
- Walking bass lines in jazz
- Modal jazz

While rock and country may dominate the airwaves in America, don't for a minute think that blues or jazz are on their way out. Comparatively, their appeal lies not in record sales, but in the fact that the music simply does something to people that's undeniable. Blues and jazz speak to people like no other music, and the bass is a huge part of both styles.

LEARNIN' THE BLUES

Before you can play the blues, you need to learn the blues. Most all blues songs are based on a standard set of chord changes known as "blues changes," or simply "blues." If someone says, "Let's play a blues in G," any musician worth his salt should know what's implied. So let's find out.

The 12-bar Form

By far the most common type of blues is the *12-bar blues*. This 12-measure progression is quite likely the most popular chord progression in pop-music history. Countless rock 'n' roll, R&B, blues, country, and jazz songs have made use of this form. Although it can be dressed up a number of ways, its most basic form involves the I, IV, and V chords. Here's the basic progression:

12-bar blues

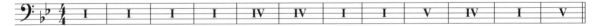

An extremely popular variation is known as a "quick-change" blues. Here, measure 2 moves to the IV chord, but everything else stays the same.

12-bar blues w/ "quick change"

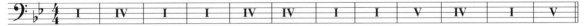

Let's see what this would look like in the key of A. Notice that all three chords (I, IV, and V) are all dominant-seventh chords. This is a common practice in blues and is largely responsible for its sound.

12-bar blues in A

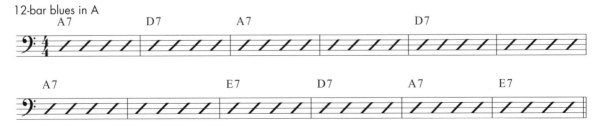

Holding Down the Bottom

The blues, like jazz, is a genre that's heavily based on improvisation. The typical blues band usually consists of a guitarist, bassist, drummer, and sometimes a keyboardist. Many times the singer (usually a guitar player or perhaps a keys player) will sing a few verses and then launch into a few choruses of an improvised solo.

A *chorus* in blues is simply one time through the entire 12-bar form. If someone takes a three-chorus solo, their solo will last 36 measures (3 × 12 = 36).

It's our job as bassists to hold down a steady groove over which the soloists can emote. You'll need to pay attention as well, because some soloists like to interact with their rhythm section by bringing the volume down or tearing the roof off the place at a moment's notice.

Using Arpeggios to Fill Out the Sound

Blues bands often take the form of trios: guitar/bass/drums, keys/bass/drums, etc. Because of this, oftentimes the bass is the only melodic instrument left accompanying the lead player during a solo. Therefore, arpeggios make an excellent choice for bass lines, as they outline the harmony and provide a more colorful backdrop for the soloist.

Here we see various approaches for the I chord in an A blues. Examples 1, 3, and 4 all make use of notes from an A7 arpeggio (A–C♯–E–G), while example 2 demonstrates a classic blues riff based on the major pentatonic scale with a chromatic note (the ♭3rd).

All of these bass lines can be transposed to the appropriate chord during the blues. For example, the A7 arpeggio shape of the third example, which takes place in fifth position, can be moved up to tenth position for the IV chord (D7) and twelfth position for the V chord (E7). Alternatively, you could simply move the shape up one string (to the A string) for the IV chord and then up two frets for the V chord.

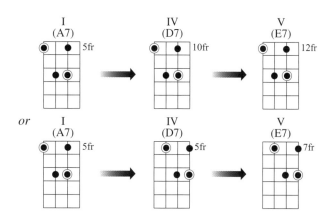

Slow Blues

Slow blues is a slightly different animal than the blues shuffle. You have much more time between chord changes, and this affords the opportunity to get a little more creative. Although you're not reinventing the wheel, there are several ways to spice up your role during these tunes.

Here we see two different approaches to the first four measures of a slow blues in A. In the first example, we combine arpeggios with chromatic passing tones for a slightly jazzy sound. The second example uses triplets on beat 4, a common rhythmic template. Remember, the dissonant-sounding E♭ notes at the end of each example are resolving down to the root of the IV chord (D7) at the very next measure.

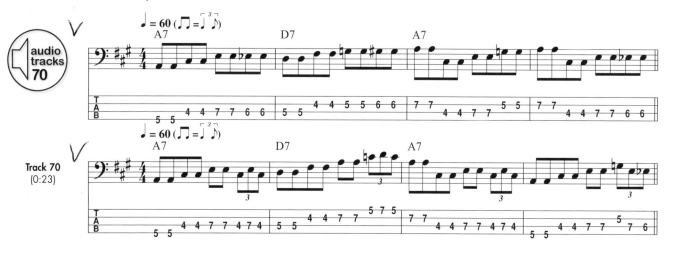

LEARN FROM THE PROS!

Let's check out some blues bass masters in action.

Pride and Joy

Hide Away

By Freddie King
and Sonny Thompson

Sweet Home Chicago

Words and Music by
Robert Johnson

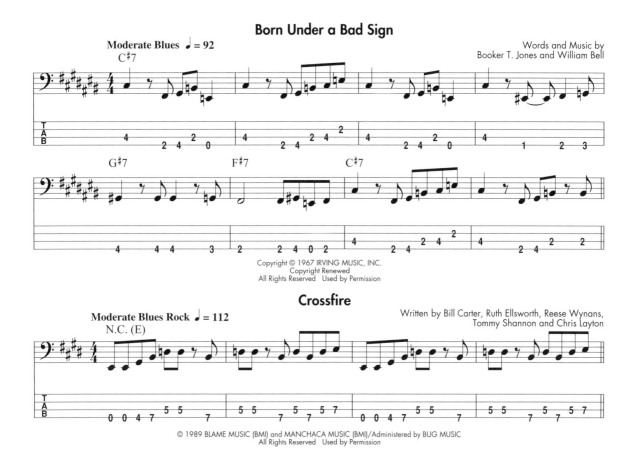

Born Under a Bad Sign

Moderate Blues ♩ = 92

Words and Music by
Booker T. Jones and William Bell

Copyright © 1967 IRVING MUSIC, INC.
Copyright Renewed
All Rights Reserved   Used by Permission

Crossfire

Moderate Blues Rock ♩ = 112

Written by Bill Carter, Ruth Ellsworth, Reese Wynans,
Tommy Shannon and Chris Layton

© 1989 BLAME MUSIC (BMI) and MANCHACA MUSIC (BMI)/Administered by BUG MUSIC
All Rights Reserved   Used by Permission

TAKING THE BASS FOR A WALK, JAZZ-STYLE

Chances are, if you ask someone to imitate jazz with their voice, they'll break into a walking bass line. The bass's role in jazz is more than essential; it's fundamental. So get out your leash and let's walk that thing!

The Blues: A Great Place to Start

Did I mention the 12-bar form was popular? Many, many jazz tunes make use of this form, as well. Jazz musicians frequently dress it up with various chord substitutions, but it often appears in its good ol' three-chord form, too. The basic walking technique consists of quarter notes. And the standard approach involves a few common practices:

- Hit the root note on the downbeat.
- Hit another chord tone on beat 2.
- Hit another chord tone or scalar tone on beat 3.
- Use the last beat to chromatically approach the next chord. (In other words, beat 4 should be a half step above or below the root of the next chord.)

If you follow these guidelines, you'll be walking in no time. Let's see how they can be applied to a blues in G. Measure 4 contains a common chord substitution you'll see in jazz-blues. This Dm7–G7 sequence is acting as a ii–V progression that leads to the forthcoming C chord in measure 5 (not shown).

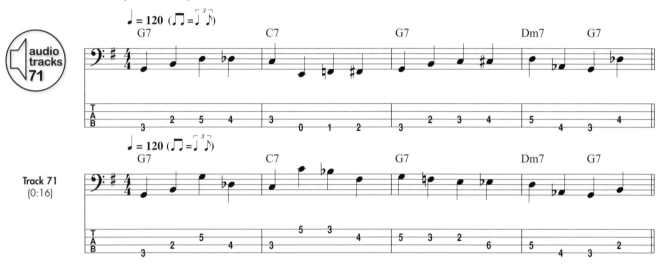

The ii–V–I–VI

Perhaps the most common progression in jazz is the ii–V–I. These three chords appear in countless jazz standards. Oftentimes, a jazz song will consist of almost nothing but ii–V–I progressions in different keys. When this progression remains in the same key and repeats, a VI chord often follows the I chord, acting as a secondary dominant to the ii chord.

> A *secondary dominant* is a non-diatonic chord that resolves down a 5th to a diatonic chord other than the I chord. For example, in C major the ii chord is usually a Dm. However, sometimes D major (or D7) is used, and it resolves down a 5th (D–C–B–A–G) to G. So the D (or D7) is a secondary dominant of G.

Let's take a look at two approaches to a ii–V–I–VI progression in the key of G. Notice that the same walking guidelines apply.

Bossa Nova

Bossa Nova is a Brazilian style that features a light, swaying-type of groove. It's become quite popular in the jazz world, and several jazz standards make use of this feel. As bassists, we get off fairly easy in this style. The typical Bossa groove consists of the root and 5th, usually with pick-up notes to each, as shown in the adjacent example.

This pattern can simply be transposed to every chord in a progression. Here's a I–ii–V progression in D major.

Track 73
(0:08)

If you encounter a chord that has an altered 5th (such as an augmented, half-diminished, etc.), simply follow suit by raising or lowering the 5th to match the chord. This ii–V–i in C minor features a Dm7♭5 chord, so the pattern makes use of A♭ instead of A to match the harmony.

Track 73
(0:22)

Modal Jazz

Throughout the '30s, '40s, and '50s, jazz improvisation grew in complexity and sophistication as soloists reached new levels of virtuosity. As players such as sax legend Charlie Parker became bored with standard chord changes, tempos rose to ridiculous heights and chord changes flew by at a blinding pace. This was *be-bop*. Eventually, this was taken about as far as it could go, and something had to give.

In the '60s, a new trend emerged. Popularized by trumpeter Miles Davis, modal jazz and the "cool school" began to take over. Tempos dipped below 200 bpm for the first time in years. In this style, the chord changes were all but eliminated. Instead, soloists played over extended one- or two-chord vamps, stretching out with various modes and chromatic material. Songs were written with modes in mind, rather than traditional major and minor keys.

The two most common modes used in this style are Dorian and Mixolydian. The bass lines in this style are often repetitive and suggestive of the mode on which they're based. This means including the characteristic scale tone that separates each mode from a standard major or minor scale.

Dorian

These bass lines are in D Dorian (D–E–F–G–A–B–C). The characteristic scale degree of the Dorian mode is the 6th tone, which is incorporated into both of the following examples.

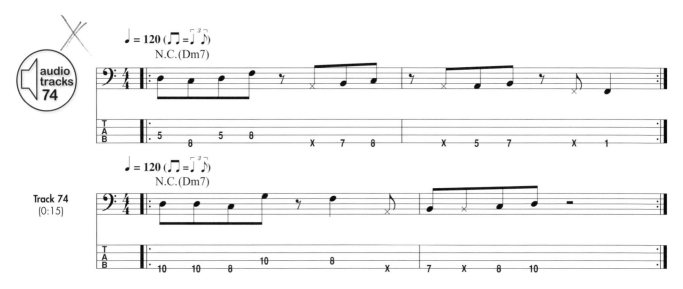

Mixolydian

Here we see two bass grooves in F Mixolydian (F–G–A–B♭–C–D–E♭). The ♭7th is what gives this mode its sound. Notice though, as the first example demonstrates, that chromatic passing tones are still an option, as well.

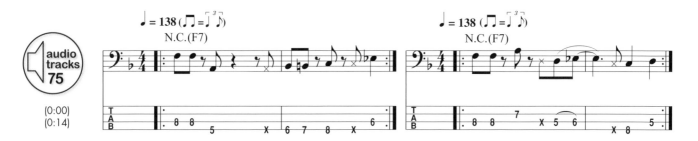

LEARN FROM THE PROS!

Now let's take a look at some of these concepts at work in real jazz songs.

Satin Doll

All the Things You Are
from VERY WARM FOR MAY

Lyrics by Oscar Hammerstein II
Music by Jerome Kern

The Girl From Ipanema
(Garôta De Ipanema)

Music by Antonio Carlos Jobim
English Words by Norman Gimbel
Original Words by Vinicius de Moraes

So What

By Miles Davis

Footprints

By Wayne Shorter

All Blues

By Miles Davis

CHAPTER 14

SHAKIN' AND GROOVIN': R&B AND FUNK STYLES

What's Ahead:
- R&B style
- Fingerstyle funk
- Slap-and-pop technique

You really haven't experienced the true joy of playing bass until you've played some R&B or funk. These two styles, in particular, contain some of the most flat-out soulful, groovin' bass playing you'll ever hear.

R&B BASS: SOULFUL TO THE CORE

The bass lines that carried the classic R&B and Motown hits of the '60s are some of the best ever. Period. Most of the bands behind the famous performers were built from some of the finest studio musicians around, and it definitely showed. Those classic tunes groove like nobody's business. At the heart of those grooves were the thumpin' bass lines from what were arguably the instrument's first virtuosos. These bass lines weren't simply supportive; they were *alive*. Sure, they grooved to no end. But they were also melodic and catchy—sometimes as catchy as the vocal melody itself!

Pentatonics: The Go-to Scale for R&B Bass

Countless classic R&B bass lines were constructed from pentatonic scales—the major pentatonic in particular. They often used repetitive pentatonic riffs to create memorable, hooky lines like the following examples. Notice in the second example how the same riff is transposed from the E chord to the B chord. This common practice is a great way to lend continuity to the groove.

Track 76
(0:14)

The slower, funkier R&B lines often made use of chromatic passing tones to embellish the major pentatonic sound. You can hear these kinds of lines in many Motown tracks. In the first example, the minor 3rd (C) is used as a chromatic approach tone to C♯, while the second example features a chromatic walk up from C♯ to E.

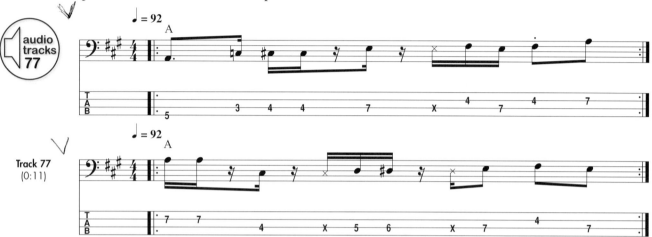

LEARN FROM THE PROS!

Check out these masterful R&B lines at work:

I Can't Help Myself
(Sugar Pie, Honey Bunch)

Words and Music by Brian Holland,
Lamont Dozier and Edward Holland

In the Midnight Hour

Words and Music by
Steve Cropper and Wilson Pickett

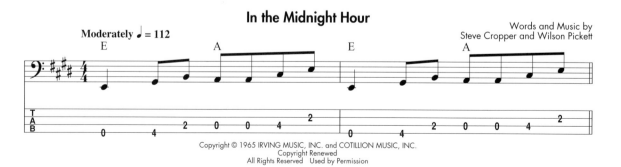

You Can't Hurry Love

Words and Music by Edward Holland,
Lamont Dozier and Brian Holland

What's Going On

Words and Music by Marvin Gaye,
Al Cleveland and Renaldo Benson

I Got You
(I Feel Good)

Words and Music by James Brown

FUNKIN' IT UP

The bass truly takes over in funk, perhaps even more so than in R&B. It almost seems as though the entire funk genre was created solely for bassists. If you wanna seriously make people move, you've got to learn how to get the funk out! There are two right-hand approaches commonly used in funk: fingerstyle and the slap-and-pop method. We'll take a look at fingerstyle first.

Fingerstyle Funk: Stamina Required!

Funk bass lines are often busy, repetitive, and relentless. This means that you've really got to have your right hand in tip-top shape. Sixteenth notes are common, and dead notes are constantly integrated as percussive time-keepers. With regard to note choice, it's usually kept fairly minimal. The root, 5th, octave, and ♭7th are common choices. The minor pentatonic is employed, too, as is the occasional chromatic passing tone.

This first example is based on the G minor pentatonic scale, with an added chromatic passing tone (F♯). Try to keep a steady sixteenth-note beat in your head throughout. This will help to keep track of the syncopated rhythms.

This line is a bit sparser, but that doesn't mean it grooves any less. Again based on G minor pentatonic, a C♯ chromatic tone sneaks its way into this line.

Slappin' and Poppin': When You Really Need to Get Funky

In the '70s, a new bass technique arrived and changed the way funk sounded forever: the *slap-and-pop technique*. This technique involves using the side of your right-hand thumb to "slap" a low string while using your right-hand first finger to "pop" the higher strings. The technique is extremely percussive sounding and is custom-made for funk's rhythmically based feel.

The Basic Technique

Your right-hand position for this technique is significantly different from your standard fingerstyle position. Try the following method for getting into position:

- Hold your right hand in a "thumbs up" position.
- Now slightly loosen your fingers so that they're not making contact with your palm.
- While holding this position, move your hand so that your first finger sits snugly underneath the top string; your thumb should be almost parallel with the third or fourth string.

This should have you in the correct starting position (see photo).

The "slap" is achieved by rotating your wrist. The side of your thumb is used to quickly slap one of the low strings and then immediately bounce off it. The motion must be quick, and it will take some practice to get it right. You should be slapping in the vicinity of the beginning of the fretboard.

The "pop" is a bit easier to achieve. Using your first finger, pull up on the string and release it, allowing it to "pop." The sound is loud, sharp, and somewhat obnoxious on its own, but it provides the perfect counterpart to the slap.

Try this first example. Play it slowly until you start to get a feel for the technique. The "T" indicates a thumb slap, while the "P" indicates a pop.

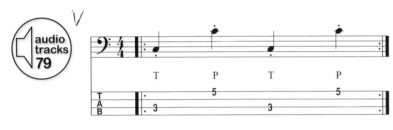

don't forget

The slap technique requires a rotation of the wrist. You shouldn't be lifting your hand up—only rotating your wrist.

Here, in the next example, the technique is put to use on a C minor pentatonic line. The riff is then extended into a C–G progression in the second example. You'll notice that you may need to employ some left-hand muting when slapping open strings to keep string noise to a minimum.

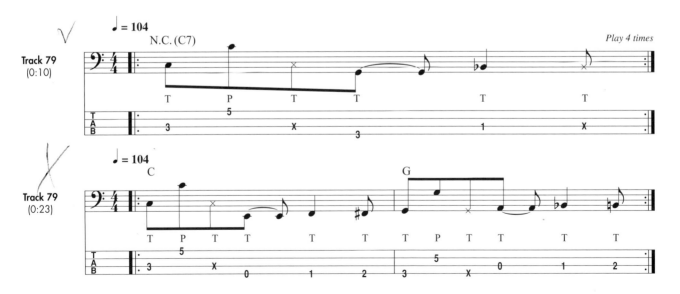

Track 79
(0:10)

Track 79
(0:23)

The Full Monty

Well, we've looked at the basic slap-and-pop technique and what it sounds like. It produces a great, unique sound that's inherently funky. But, there's much more to the technique than the basics. There's a whole percussive part of this technique that needs to be learned in order to really hear what it can do.

Several percussive dead notes and clicks are used in more advanced slap-and-pop riffs. There are basically three sounds: the dead-note thumb slap, the dead-note pop, and the dead-note left-hand slap.

For the dead-note thumb slap and dead-note pop, all you need to do is simply perform the right-hand action while laying your left hand lightly across the strings, just as when performing a normal dead note. For the left-hand slap, you use the left hand to quickly and lightly slap the strings to create a click sound. This needs to be forceful enough to make a noise, but not so forceful as to actually fret a note. It's kind of a like a hammer-on that doesn't quite make it.

Here are the three percussive sounds performed back to back to back as a triplet figure. Practice this slowly, and gradually build up speed to match the tempo on the CD. The "L" indicates the dead-note left-hand slap.

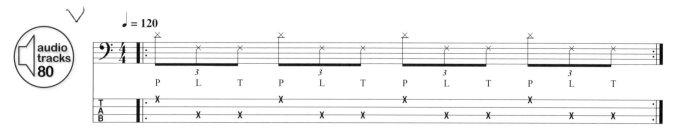

Next, we've doubled up on the dead-note thumb slaps to create a four-note pattern. It's important to be able to perform any of these actions on any part of the beat. The following examples feature the same four-note sequence, but the pop is shifted one sixteenth note each time. You're always performing the same thumb-thumb-pop-left sequence, but it's falling on different divisions of the beat.

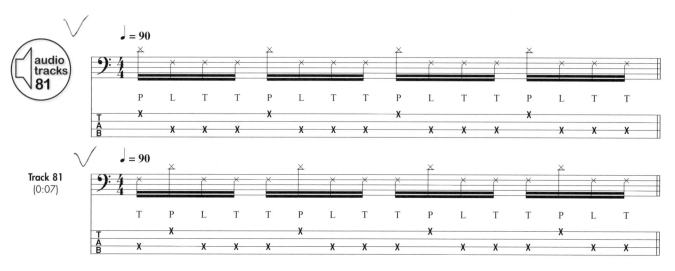

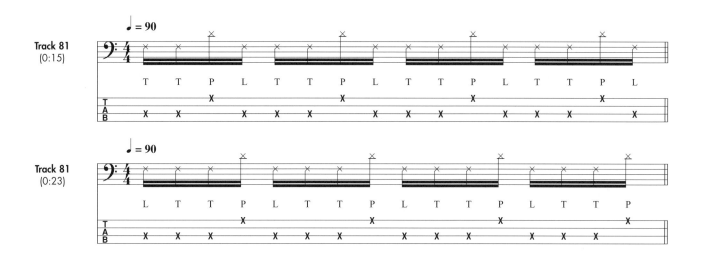

Now let's hear how these can be used in some actual lines. The first two are E Dorian lines that include a few hammer-ons. The third example is derived from the D Dorian mode and makes use of some pull-offs, slides, hammer-ons, and a left-hand "hammer-on from nowhere" at the end of measure 1. You sound this G note by forcefully hammering on with your second finger.

The last riff is from the A minor pentatonic scale and makes use of all three percussive sounds back to back again.

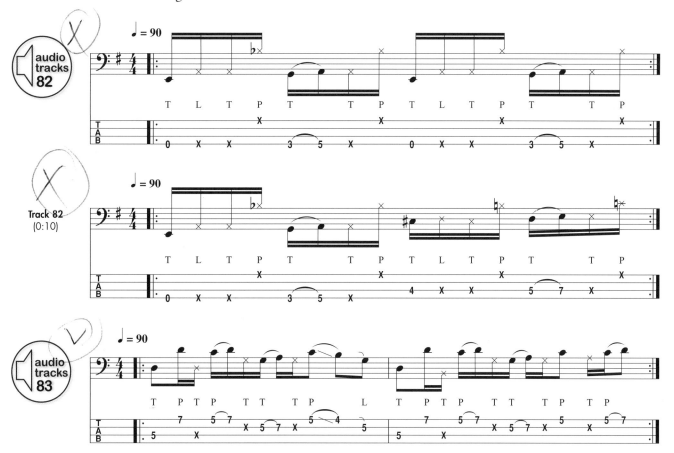

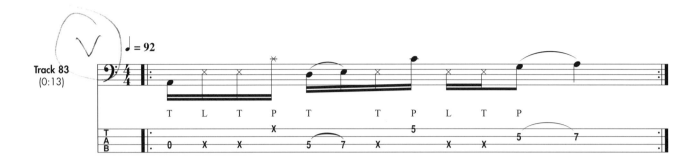

LEARN FROM THE PROS!

Let's hear how the professional funkmasters get it done.

Get Up (I Feel Like Being) A Sex Machine

Words and Music by James Brown,
Bobby Byrd and Ronald Lenhoff

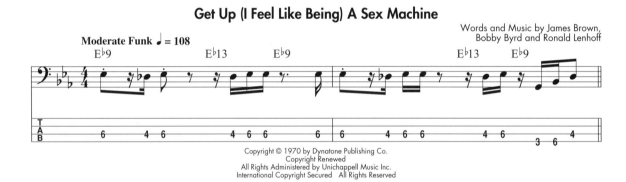

Brick House

Words and Music by Lionel Richie, Ronald LaPread,
Walter Orange, Milan Williams,
Thomas McClary and William King

Love and Happiness

Words and Music by
Al Green and Mabon Hodges

Knock on Wood

Words and Music by
Eddie Floyd and Steve Cropper

Higher Ground

Words and Music by
Stevie Wonder

Far-out Stuff

CHAPTER 15
SPECIAL EFFECTS AND TECHNIQUES

What's Ahead:
- False harmonics
- Finger tapping
- String bending
- Foam at the bridge

While we bassists generally stick to keeping the bottom steady and providing the foundation, we've still got a few tricks up our sleeve that we can pull out at the right time. Let's take a look at a few.

FALSE (ARTIFICIAL) HARMONICS

Don't worry—these harmonics aren't frauds or anything like that. They're known as false harmonics because they don't naturally occur along the bass strings. They require the combination of both of your hands along the string to make them work.

The adjacent example demonstrates this technique. While fretting the A note on fret 7, lightly place your right-hand thumb over fret 19. Now use another right-hand finger to pluck the string, removing your thumb immediately afterwards. You should end up with a chime that's one octave higher than the fretted note. These are also called *harp harmonics*, hence the "H.H." used in the notation.

If using your right-hand thumb to produce the harmonic feels too awkward, you can try using your right-hand first finger in its place.

Here we use the technique to play an A minor pentatonic scale.

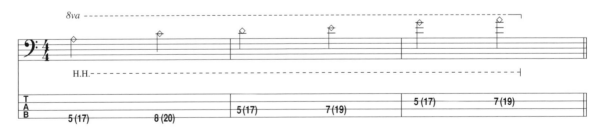

Track 84
(0:08)

While this technique may feel extremely cumbersome and awkward in the beginning, it can actually be used to add another dimension to some of your lines. In the next example, which is derived from the A minor pentatonic scale, the false harmonics create a tone that's similar to a Fender Rhodes. The example that follows chimes its way down a second-inversion A chord in measure 2.

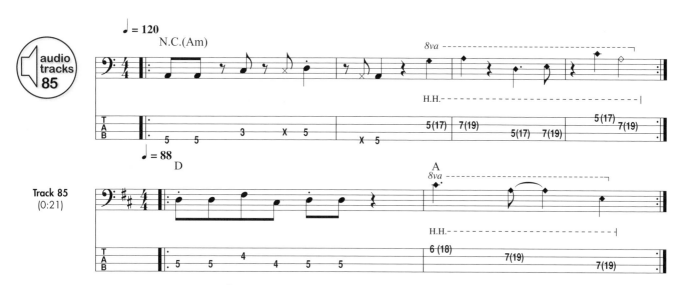

FINGER TAPPING: WHO SAYS IT'S ONLY FOR GUITARISTS?

OK, so Eddie Van Halen got to it first. That doesn't mean it's off limits to us. Finger tapping is a great way to sound flashy without too much difficulty.

The basic technique involves simultaneously using both your right and left hands on the fretboard to hammer on and pull off notes. You can achieve a great deal of speed fairly quickly with this technique, and it sounds much more difficult than it actually is—and that's always a good thing.

Just as you did with your left hand, you'll develop soreness in your tapping finger when you first start out. If you decide to permanently add the technique to your arsenal, you'll eventually develop a callous on that finger, as well. However, make sure to not overdo it in the beginning!

Here's a good basic lick with which to get started. We're playing the notes of a G major arpeggio, but we're doing it all on one string. Plant the first and fourth fingers of your left hand on frets 4 and 7, respectively. Start the lick by "tapping" onto the twelfth fret with your right-hand first finger, and then pull off to your left-hand fourth finger at fret 7. Continue with another pull-off, this time to your first finger at fret 4.

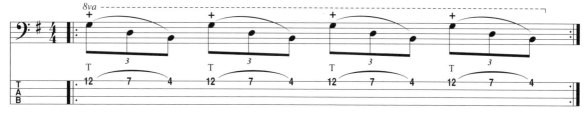

Here we're reversing the order of the left-hand notes. You'll probably find this a bit easier than the first one.

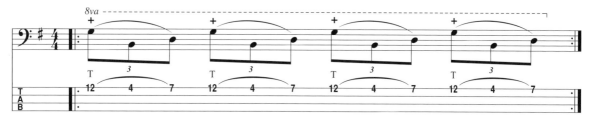

Next, we'll add another left-hand note to create more of a scalar sound. This type of lick can sound really impressive at fast tempos.

Track 86
(0:21)

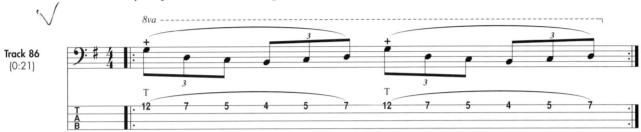

In this last one, we're using the same four notes, but this time in a sixteenth-note rhythm. We're also alternating the direction of the left-hand notes.

Track 86
(0:31)

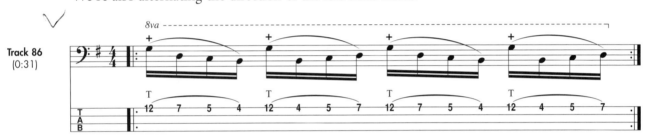

As you can see, the limits of this technique will not be reached anytime soon. Check out virtuosos Billy Sheehan and Stuart Hamm for a taste of what can really be done with finger tapping.

STRING BENDING

If you've hung around guitarists at all, you've probably seen them bending strings left and right (unless it's a classical guitarist). This is a very expressive technique that's used to great effect in blues, but we bassists can get in on the fun, too. The thicker string gauge on a bass makes it less practical than on a guitar, but it's still manageable.

When you bend a string, the pitch goes up. The farther you bend it, the higher the pitch rises. On the bass, the most practical bends are half-step bends and whole-step bends. In a half-step bend, you're bending the equivalent of one half step (or one fret). In a whole-step bend, you're bending the equivalent of one whole step (or two frets).

audio tracks 87

Let's take a look at the basic technique with a half-step bend on the second string. In this example, fret the A note with your third finger and use your first and second fingers behind it for support. Play the note, and then push the string up (toward the ceiling) until the pitch matches a B♭ note.

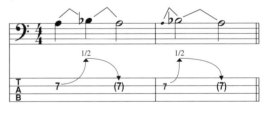

try this

When you're first starting out, it's a good idea to check your pitch by playing the first note and then playing the target note. For instance, in the previous example, play the A note and then the B♭ note at fret 8 to hear the pitch to which you're bending.

Here's a whole-step bend on the first string.

Track 87
(0:11)

don't forget

> Bending takes a good deal of left-hand strength, so be sure to support your bending finger with the others behind it. You may not be able to stretch the string far enough at first, but with practice, you'll develop the required strength.

Now let's check out some of these bends in action. The first two examples make use of half-step bends, while the last one uses two different whole-step bends.

audio tracks 88

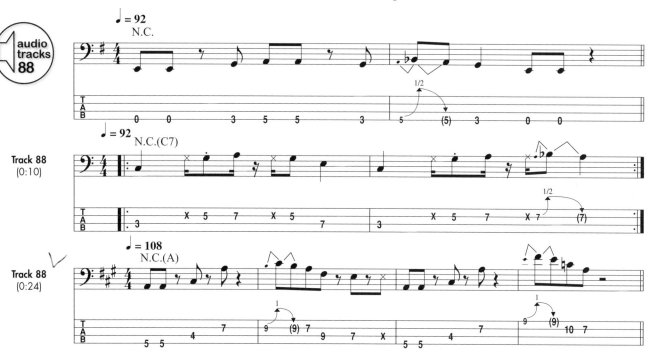

Track 88
(0:10)

Track 88
(0:24)

FOAM AT THE BRIDGE

Here's something you can try to get a unique tone from your bass. By cramming a piece of foam under your strings right next to the bridge, you can achieve a thumping, percussive tone that's slightly reminiscent of an upright bass.

When the electric bass was first marketed in the early '50s, they were actually shipped with a piece of foam in this spot. Perhaps this was because, after hearing the sustain-less tone of an upright bass for so long, the full, unmuted sound of the electric bass was a bit too much. At any rate, it's a great tone with which to experiment when you want that early R&B type of sound.

If you can't get your hands on a piece of foam, you can use other items, as well. Just about anything that mutes the strings will work—a towel, a sock (a clean one!), a sponge, etc. Some things may work better than others, but you'll achieve the same basic effect.

Here's an example of what it sounds like. Notice that the sustain is substantially decreased, but the notes "thump" a bit more.

CHAPTER 16

CHAPTER 16
MORE OPTIONS: EXTENDED RANGE, ALTERNATE TUNING, AND OTHER BASSES

> **What's Ahead:**
> - Fretless bass
> - Extended-range basses (five- and six-strings and beyond)
> - Alternate tunings
> - The Chapman stick

The standard four-string bass is certainly worthy of life-long study, but some players feel the need to expand their options. Whether it's through extended range with extra strings or alternate tunings, the tonal variation of a fretless, or the two-handed possibilities of the Chapman Stick, there are plenty of ways to keep the low end interesting.

FRETLESS BASS

A fretless bass is just what it sounds like: a bass without frets. Fretless basses are made, as well as converted from fretted models. Some models have lines across the fingerboard (it's not a *fretboard* anymore!) where the frets would go, but many models have nothing but a blank fingerboard.

With a fretless bass, the tuning of every note depends on you! In order to develop your intonation, it's best to practice along with another instrument or with a CD so you have something against which to reference your pitches.

fretless bass neck

fretless bass neck with fret markers

try this

If you have the means, here's a great way to work on your intonation: Record yourself playing a bass line on a standard bass, and then play along to that recording with your fretless. Be very discriminating when it comes to matching the pitch. Don't stop until you can hardly hear a difference between the two instruments.

The tone of a fretless is very smooth and distinct. Slides really come to life on a fretless since, due to the lack of frets, you can achieve a true *glissando* (slide). Listen to the smooth sound of the slide on this next example.

A common practice with the fretless bass is to play sliding *double stops*, as heard in the next example. The term *double stop* is simply a fancy name for playing two notes simultaneously.

Many bassists like to include a fretless in their collection for those times when that tone is desired. Although a standard bass will get the job done 95 percent of the time, when you want *that* tone, nothing else but a fretless will do.

EXTENDED-RANGE BASSES

Basses that contain more than four strings are known as *extended-range basses*. The most common extended-range is the five-string, but six-, seven-, and eight-strings are occasionally used, as well. Each extended-range bass expands upon the same four strings found on a standard bass by adding strings above or below.

Here's a breakdown of their additions to the standard four-string format:

Five-string:
added low B string

Six-string:
added low B string
and high C string

Seven-string:
six-string with an
added high F string

The added range of a five-string allows your lines to reach new groove depths, redefining what's known as "bottom end." Check out these five-string examples to hear the added range in action.

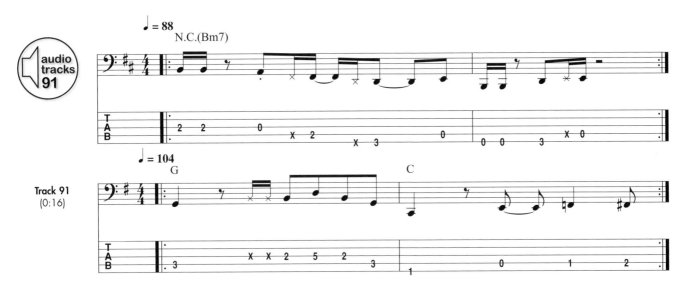

Six-strings and above are most popular in the realm of bass soloists, as they afford the ability to better explore the upper range. Jazz/fusion master John Patitucci comes to mind in this regard.

ALTERNATE TUNINGS

Though the E–A–D–G tuning system is the standard, it's not set in stone. Players occasionally employ *alternate tunings* to achieve certain results otherwise not possible. An *alternate tuning* is created when one or more strings are tuned to a note other than standard. Any string can be tuned differently, but the fourth string is the most common choice.

Here are some reasons why alternate tunings are used:

- **To get a heavier sound**: Many newer metal and hard-rock bands, in their quest for ultra-heaviness, have adopted the practice of tuning down. This can include just the bottom string or sometimes all four strings.
- **To facilitate a certain riff**: Sometimes we need to play a certain riff that simply won't sound as good in standard tuning. Perhaps an open string is needed, but the standard open strings don't fit with the song's key.
- **To temporarily extend the range**: Sometimes the fourth string is tuned down a whole step or more, allowing a few lower notes to be reached at some point during the song.

Drop D (D–A–D–G)

The most common alternate tuning is known as *Drop D*. To get into Drop D tuning, you only need to lower your fourth string by a whole step. Since your second string is a D note, simply match the fourth string to it. (The fourth string will be an octave lower than the second string.)

This tuning is fun because it allows you access to a low D but keeps all the other strings the same, so you don't have to relearn the fretboard. Songs in the key of D are obviously quite common in this tuning. Check out the examples on the following page.

Drop D tuning:
(low to high) D–A–D–G

♩ = 80

N.C.(D5)

Drop D tuning:
(low to high) D–A–D–G

♩ = 80

N.C.(D5)

Track 92
(0:17)

Other Tunings

There are a number of other tunings to explore. Here's a quick list to get you started. Each one will afford certain riffs that wouldn't otherwise be possible.

- E–G–D–G
- D–G–D–G
- D–G–C–F (whole step below standard)
- C–A–D–G
- C–G–D–G
- C–G–C–G

Keep in mind that some tunings (especially the low C tunings) will probably work better with thicker string gauges. If you're going to make a habit of playing in a dropped tuning, you may want to switch gauges.

THE CHAPMAN STICK

No, Charlie Chapman wasn't a bass player (at least not that I know of). The Chapman stick is an instrument created by Emmett Chapman in the early '70s. It's an odd-looking instrument that resembles a large fretboard without a body. There are a number of different variations, but the standard "stick" consists of 10 strings: five for bass and five for melody.

The Chapman stick is played exclusively by tapping on the fretboard with both hands. It's possible to play a bass line with the left hand while tapping melodies and/or chords with the right. It has become quite popular among bassists, as the tone of the bass strings is quite unique. Tony Levin has made use of this device on some Peter Gabriel recordings, as has Greg Howard of the Dave Matthews Band.

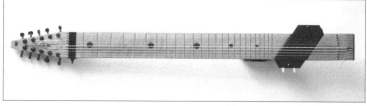

Photo courtesy of Colin Nicholls

SECTION **6**

Jammin' With the Pros

CHAPTER 17
FULL-SONG TRANSCRIPTIONS

> **What's Ahead:**
> - "All I Wanna Do"
> - "Message in a Bottle"
> - "Sweet Emotion"
> - "I Want You Back"
> - "Cissy Strut"

This is the fun part of the book. Here we get to see everything come together in full-length transcriptions of five hits. Enjoy!

"ALL I WANNA DO"

A relaxed groove propels this early '90s Sheryl Crow hit, and the bass line follows suit with a fairly sparse approach that combines a few well-placed riffs with a solid root/5th style. The tone is round, mellow, and full, with not much attack. If you're having trouble getting the sound, you might try rolling your tone knob off a little.

The main hammer-on riff in the verse is transposed up an octave for the chorus—a clever arranging device that helps set apart the sections. (An octave pedal is also engaged here for a thickening effect.) Notice that the chord progression is essentially the same in both sections. The chorus concludes with a great eighth-note lick in which descending notes from the E minor pentatonic scale are pivoted against the open A string.

The pre-chorus is particularly interesting. Here, the bass riffs on A minor pentatonic throughout, somewhat disregarding the B♭7 chord change. Notice, however, that the D note that occurs on this B♭7 change is the 3rd of B♭. So the riff functions on two levels: both as a catchy A minor pentatonic riff, and as an inversion over the B♭ chord.

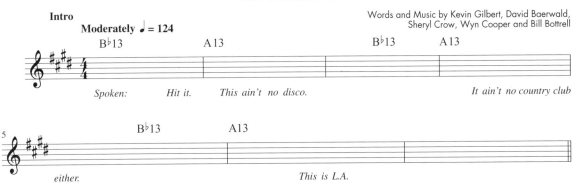

Santa Mon - i - ca Bou - le - vard,_____ un - til the

sun comes up o - ver San - ta Mon - i - ca Bou - le - vard._____

*Sing 1st time only.

"MESSAGE IN A BOTTLE"

The Police classic "Message in a Bottle" cruises along at a brisk rock tempo and makes use of three distinct feels throughout. Sting's lines are deliberate, thoughtful, and deliver just what the song needs.

For the verse, in support of the vocals and highly syncopated guitar riff, the bass line sticks to roots to keep it simple. Don't disregard the slide down from the first C# note of each phrase. It's these subtle touches that add life to music.

The chorus changes gears to a steady eighth-note approach, though the V chord (E) appears on the "and" of beat 2. Otherwise, there's no syncopation to be found. This is a wonderful example of how to utilize contrast in an arrangement to maintain interest. For the last part of the chorus (the "message in a bottle" line), a catchy riff that combines straight quarter notes in one measure with a syncopated approach in the next takes over. The part is made even more interesting with the pseudo half-time feel of the drums.

Message in a Bottle

Music and Lyrics by Sting

Additional Lyrics

2. A year has passed since I wrote my note.
   I should have know this right from the start.
   Only hope can keep me together.
   Love can mend your life, but love can break your heart.

3. Woke up this morning, I don't believe what I saw,
   Hundred billion bottles washed up on the shore.
   Seems I never noticed being alone.
   Hundred billion castaways, looking for a home,

"SWEET EMOTION"

This Aerosmith classic opens with one of the most recognizable bass riffs in all of rock. Tom Hamilton works within the A Mixolydian mode (A–B–C#–D–E–F#–G) in the upper register, pivoting the tonic A note at the twelfth fret of the A string against higher syncopated notes to create a grooving and extremely catchy line. This is used to support the chorus, as well.

The verse is essentially a one-chord jam on A5. While the guitars riff loosely around A5 with notes from the A minor pentatonic, the bass sticks to mostly roots in different positions, working from the same basic syncopated framework as the guitars. For the interlude, the bass doubles the guitars for the classic, syncopated, chromatically tinged riff. Later in the song, Hamilton joins the guitars during the verse, doubling the A minor pentatonic riff.

For the outro, which centers on an E tonality, Hamilton creates a line that's very similar to the intro/chorus riff. However, it's heard in the lowest register (in the key of E) this time, so the similarity isn't entirely obvious. Nevertheless, the thematic unity is unquestionably inferred by the listener.

Outro
N.C.(E7)   *Play 12 times and fade*

Additional Lyrics

3. I pulled into town in a police car;
   You daddy said I took you just a little too far.
   You're tellin' her things but your girlfriend lied:
   You can't catch me 'cause the rabbit done died.

4. You can't catch me 'cause the rabbit done died.
   I'll take you backstage, you can drink from my glass.
   I'm talkin' 'bout somethin' you can sure understand,
   'Cause a month on the road and I'll be eatin' from your hand.

"I WANT YOU BACK"

This soulful R&B classic from the Jackson Five contains a seriously grooving bass line from start to finish. With sixteenth notes abounding, it's a fairly difficult line and will most likely take a while to work up. Remember to start slowly and gradually increase the tempo. The tone in this piece is round and thumpin'; using foam near the bridge will help to replicate it.

The intro line is brilliant. With its use of chromatic passing tones and syncopated sixteenth-note runs, it simply steals the show. This line ends up supporting the verse, as well. The second half of the intro features a line that descends through the A♭ major scale, creating a few inversions (E♭/G and D♭/C) along the way. The line is rhythmically active as well, and contains a bit of syncopation on beat 3 of each measure. Notice again the use of chromatic passing tones at the end of measure 7 and the classic major-pentatonic fill at the end of measure 9.

The descending line supports the chorus as well, and the section is concluded with the sixteenth-note ensemble figure in support of the "I want you back" lyric. The bridge gives you an arpeggio work out, as Fm, Cm, D♭, and A♭ arpeggios are all combined in one fluid syncopated riff.

I Want You Back

Words and Music by Freddie Perren,
Alphonso Mizell, Berry Gordy and Deke Richards

Additional Lyrics

2. Tryin' to live without your love is one long sleepless night.
   Let me show you, girl, that I know wrong from right.
   Every street you walk on, I leave tear stains on the ground.
   Followin' the girl I didn't even want around. Let me tell you, now.

"CISSY STRUT"

The Meters laid down the funk, New Orleans-style, in the late '60s with a number of instrumental hits, including the Top 10 "Cissy Strut." This severely danceable track is largely built upon a one-chord groove utilizing a swung sixteenth-note feel with serious stress on the *groove*.

The main riff opens with a Cm7 arpeggio and a sassy, quarter-step bend on the E♭. The tonality primarily used throughout the song is C Dorian (C–D–E♭–F–G–A–B♭), as evidenced by the low A note in the main riff. With so little in the way of harmonic complexity, the success of this tune rests squarely on attitude and the strength of the groove. At measure 9, we find the only departure from the Dorian tonality: the low open E string (major 3rd), which provides a nice contrast and helps to avoid monotony.

Remember to make those sixteenth notes nice and lopsided to accentuate the swing feel. This is the key to making this song groove.

Cissy Strut

By Arthur Neville, Leo Nocentelli,
George Porter, and Joseph Modeliste, Jr.

The Gig

CHAPTER 18
RULE #1: BE PREPARED!

What's Ahead:
- The gig checklist
- The virtues of punctuality
- Making the best of your soundcheck
- Warming up
- Tune!
- Know your stuff!

The thought may scare the wits out of some, while it may dangle in front of others like a hundred-dollar bill on a string. At some point, you're going to have your first gig. (The word "gig" is serious musician lingo, so get used to it!) You're going to have to get up on stage and show people what you've got. Whether it's in front of five people (which is very possible!) or 100, you're more than likely going to be a bit nervous, so it's a good thing you bought this book. There are a number of things that you can do to make sure you're in the best possible shape for this inevitable situation.

MAKE A LIST!

When you're nervous before a show, you're not thinking clearly. It's very easy to forget things in this state of mind. So it's essential that you think ahead and make a list of everything you need while you're calm and collected. Believe me—as crazy as it sounds, it's not unheard of for a bassist to head off to a gig without his bass!

Depending on your personal needs, this may not be a comprehensive list, but it should be a very good start. If you're not entirely sure what all this stuff is, consult Section 8 for more on gear.

The obvious:
- bass
- amplifier
- cable
- effects pedals (if applicable)

The not-so-obvious:
- tuner
- back-up bass (beg, borrow, or do whatever you have to do to acquire a back-up bass! They're lifesavers!)
- bass stand(s)
- extra cables
- fresh batteries (for pedals, etc.)
- fresh strings (several sets)
- extra fuses and/or tubes (for amplifier)
- picks (if you use them)
- tool kit (see Chapter 22)
- power strip/extension cords
- extra strap
- duct tape

- ear plugs
- pen and paper
- DI box ("direct injection"—used for plugging an instrument directly into a mixer)
- small flashlight
- music/charts
- towel (you'll probably sweat on stage!)
- promotional materials (CDs, mailing list, flyers, business cards, etc.)

The really not-so-obvious:
- change for parking meter (if needed)
- extra cash
- change of clothes or an extra shirt (are you going somewhere after the gig?)

There are certainly other factors involved that may substantially increase or decrease this list. For instance, if you're supplying your own P.A. (stands for "public announcement"—powered amplifier with speaker cabinets), your list will certainly get longer. You'll have to use your imagination and try to think of anything you may need. Experience is certainly a great teacher, but you can save yourself a lot of trouble if you just think ahead.

FASHIONABLY LATE IS NOT THE WAY TO GO!

It may be cool for parties, but being late to a gig is a huge no-no. You may not get to soundcheck, but you'll put your band in a huge bind if you're still not there when it's time to perform. Murphy's Law loves musicians, so expect the unexpected on gig day. Treat your gigs like you're told to treat your flight experiences: show up several hours early, if possible.

Remember that unloading gear takes time, especially if the venue is already crowded, and allow time for dealing with disgruntled club owners, bouncers, etc. Don't be surprised when you hear, "You can't park there," and be prepared to do something about it. All of those little things take time, and time flies when you're in a rush.

The Squeaky Wheel Gets the Grease!

If you encounter a problem during soundcheck, speak up! Don't be shy. The soundperson (who's usually provided by the club when it comes to small local bands) doesn't really have any stake in whether or not you sound great. He's not going to go out of his way to make you feel like a diva. Occasionally, you'll run into a very attentive soundperson, but many times they won't even say a word to you except, "Ok...guitar. OK, got it. Now bass. OK, got it..."

It's up to you to let them know that you can't hear your vocals. If the guitar is too loud in your monitor, let them know. If the drums are... well... never mind—drummers are always too loud!

HAVE A PRODUCTIVE SOUNDCHECK

Usually bands are given a brief period on stage to check the sound system after everyone has been miked up and plugged in. This is referred to as *soundcheck*. National touring bands have the luxury of several hours or more, but local unknown bands are lucky to get ten minutes—if that! This means you have to make the most of the time you have.

Get together with your band members and decide on a song that allows you to get the most bang for your soundcheck buck. If you have back-up vocalists in your band, make sure the song allows them to check their microphone levels. If you use certain effects with your bass rig, try them out during the soundcheck song, even if you normally don't use them for that song. Sometimes bands write songs solely for the purpose of soundchecks.

Take the opportunity during soundcheck to get acclimated to your stage position, as well. Move around a little; loosen up. Remember, there's no pressure yet. Use the time to try and relax and remember that you're supposed to be having fun.

ZEN AND THE ART OF WARMING UP

If you're like me, you're going to have trouble getting your fingers on the right strings minutes before your first gig, much less worrying about grooving hard. But, if that's the case, then it's probably because, like me, you didn't warm up properly before said gig. It's very easy, with all the hoopla going on beforehand, to skip the warm-up. You helped your drummer carry his drums in. The guitar player needed an extra cable, so you helped him out. Your friend, whom you haven't seen in months, showed up early, so you gabbed with him. Before you know it, you get the signal from your singer that it's time to go on.

Essentially, this is like an Olympic runner changing from his street clothes minutes before a race, walking up to the starting line, and not bending his legs until he gets in the "set" position. OK, so playing bass isn't exactly like running in the Olympics, but you get my point. Besides the fact that playing music is a physical activity and you're ideally supposed to stretch before any prolonged physical activity, there are many other factors at play.

> If you suffer from stage fright, even slightly, warming up can greatly benefit you. It stops your mind from wandering and your anxiety from compounding. So learn from my mistake! Try to make it a ritual to set aside 20 or 30 minutes or so for any or all of the following activities. It really can make a world of difference.

Stretch out: Take a few minutes and get limber (see Chapter 2). This will get your blood flowing and help to ease your tension.

Breathe: Take some deep, cleansing breaths and remember that you're supposed to be having fun. Try visualizing yourself on stage playing great and having a blast.

Play scales: After you've stretched, play something simple like scales or arpeggios, and play them solidly and authoritatively. This helps to calm the pre-show jitters that crop up often when you're new to the stage. And don't forget to breathe!

Play songs from your repertoire or other favorites: Hopefully, you've come prepared for this gig. You shouldn't be using this time to "cram" like you used to before your final exams in school. You should take the time to get your riffs and lines well under your fingers before you're ready to go on stage. This time should be just for fun; you're just playing some songs.

GET IN TUNE!

Make sure all of your basses are in tune before the first downbeat. If something goes wrong and you have to move to a back-up bass, you don't want to have to worry about whether or not it's in tune.

DO YOUR HOMEWORK

Lastly, but certainly not least, *know your stuff*. This is perhaps one of the most important things of all. With everything else in this chapter, you could technically luck out. You may hit no traffic and have no trouble parking, soundcheck could go smoothly, and you may not have any technical difficulties whatsoever. However, if you don't know your stuff, you're in trouble.

Hello, Autopilot!

When that first song is counted off, you'll probably encounter your first out-of-body experience. It's not uncommon for people to say they can't remember the first few songs after their first gig. You're pretty much going to be running on autopilot, and "grooving" is not really going to be the top priority in your mind. Here are a few things that may be rushing through your head after the first song starts:

- Holy crap! I'm on stage!
- This sounds really weird up here!
- Is everyone staring at me?
- Is my fly zipped?
- I can't see anything with these lights in my eyes!
- I can't move my right leg!

When you're in this state, your muscle memory takes over and says, "OK, brain, if you're not going to help, I guess I'm going to have to do this myself." In other words, you need to have your stuff down cold. During those first few songs, you're not going to be able to count on extreme concentration to get you through. Count on not knowing what the heck is happening!

After a few songs, you'll usually be able to catch your breath a little, and you may start to settle down a bit. Before that, though, you really have to rely on those hours and hours of preparation. Know your stuff backwards and forwards!

CHAPTER 19

UNDER THE LIMELIGHT: WHAT TO EXPECT ON STAGE

> **What's Ahead:**
> * Feeling at home on the bandstand
> * Dealing with trouble

So you've practiced in your room for countless hours. You've booked your first gig and told everyone and their mother about it. You've read Chapter 18 and you arrived early, warmed up, and are good to go. And you step onto the stage...

I'M ON STAGE—NOW WHAT?

Depending on the venue, your first experience "on stage" can vary greatly from one person to the next. Your first "stage" could be the patio next to someone's backyard pool or a driveway during a block party. It could even be a real stage that's risen off of the floor with stage lights and everything! No matter where it's located, the point is that you're the entertainment and people have come (maybe even paid!) to see you.

Stage Etiquette

Regardless of whether your main concern is sounding great, looking cool, or both, you need to come to grips with the fact that the stage is going to be your home for the next 40 minutes or so. Here are some things to keep in mind to help it go smoothly.

Be aware of your surroundings: Preferably before you start to play, take a look around you and your area of the stage. Getting acquainted with your available space can help prevent you from knocking your drummer's cymbals over or stepping on your guitar player's (or your own) cable.

Remember your role: If you're not the singer, you're usually not the "frontman." This means that your place is part of the grooving rhythm section. Trying to compete for attention with the lead singer is counterproductive and will most likely look awkward and confusing to the audience. You can look coolest simply by laying down the groove.

Make eye contact with your band members: This is not only important for catching certain rhythmic hits and the like, but it also helps to settle you down a bit. You've (hopefully) played these songs many times before this gig, and seeing your band members will help you remember that.

Don't be a statue: As soon as you regain feeling in your legs (if it's your first gig), loosen up a bit. If nothing else, start by tapping your foot. Shake what your momma gave ya! Moving with the music will help set the audience at ease and will probably make you groove better, as well.

Don't endlessly noodle between songs: If other members are trying to tune, or if someone's trying to talk to the audience, this can be very distracting.

Frequently check your tuning: If you're going to be playing gigs often, you've got to get a tuner that will allow you to quickly check your tuning. This means it needs to be in your signal path so you don't have to unplug your cable and plug into it. Any time you've got 20 seconds or so (between songs, for example), check to see if you've slipped out of tune. Pedal tuners work great because when you engage them your sound does not pass through to your amp. You can see if you're in tune, but the audience doesn't have to listen to: *slightly flat A... not-quite-as-flat A... almost-in-tune A... in-tune A.*

Use a metronome! Have your drummer use a metronome with a flashing light. Usually these models will allow you to turn the sound off. This way, he can set the metronome for the tempo of the song without hearing "beep, beep, beep." Musicians tend to rush the tempo quite a bit when they're new to the stage and the adrenaline's pumping. A metronome can help tame that problem.

HOUSTON, WE HAVE A PROBLEM

If you're like the majority of us, there's going to be some point when you run into trouble of some kind on stage. There are a number of things that can go wrong, and there's usually a simple solution to be found. Let's take a look at some common problems.

No Sound

You're going along fine and then... no bass! Where'd my sound go? Check the following, in this order:

Volume control: Did your volume somehow get rolled off?

Unplugged cable: Check your instrument end, the amp end, and any cables connecting pedals, etc.

Amplifier off: Does your amp have power? If not, did the switch get flicked? Did the power cord come unplugged? If the switch is still on, the amp's plugged in, and you have no power, you probably have a blown fuse. Learn how to replace the fuse in your amp (before the gig) and always have spares on hand.

Bad battery: If you use pedals with batteries, one of them could have given out. (Use fresh batteries at every show!)

Broken String

If you're not fortunate enough to have a roadie that will run out and hand you another bass the minute you've got trouble, a broken string can be a pain. The problem with broken strings is that it will usually throw the rest of your instrument out of tune, which is why playing the rest of the song with the other available strings is not always an option. Here's how to handle a broken string (see Chapter 23 for how to change strings):

If it happens to be the last song in the set:

- Engage your pedal tuner, check your tuning (with no sound coming from your amp), and get through the rest of the song with the remaining strings. Change the strings on your set break. (Remember to stretch out the strings well!)

- If you don't have a pedal tuner, roll off your volume and fake it through the rest of the song. Change the strings during the set break.

If it's not the last song in the set:

- If you have a back-up bass, grab it, quickly check the tuning, and join back in.

- If you don't have a back-up bass, you're in trouble. Your only real options are to re-tune and ride it out with your remaining strings or perform the fastest string change of your life. Occasionally, a bassist from another band may lend his bass to you, but don't count on this happening.

Drawing a Blank

When you're very new to the stage, it's possible that your nervousness can get the best of you. Sometimes you simply forget the song. It's not the end of the world, and it usually doesn't last long. Here's how to ride it through while doing the least amount of damage:

If you forget the lyrics:

- If you're the lead singer and forget the lyrics, just make some dummy lyric sounds that somewhat resemble the real words. A lot of times it's very difficult to make out the words during live shows anyway, so it's likely that no one (except maybe your band) will even notice. If you continue to draw blanks after several lines, ask your band for a clue.
- If you're a harmony singer and forget the lyrics, just wait one second and listen to the lead. It will come back to you right away.

If you forget the chord progression/riff:

- If you forget what you're supposed to play, try not to panic. Play some dead notes for a few beats or measures until you find your place again. If you're having trouble remembering a complicated riff, just play the root note until it comes back to you. If you're completely lost, try looking at the guitar player to see where his fingers are located.

Even though it may feel like it, not everyone's eyes are on you while you're on stage. This is especially true if you're not the lead singer. Many times little mistakes that may get you very frustrated go completely unnoticed by everyone in the audience.

A Shocking Issue

Hopefully, you'll never be exposed to this, but it's unlikely. You accidentally touch the microphone with your mouth and *Bzzz!* You get a shock. It's a horrible feeling with somewhat lasting repercussions. It will make you fearful of stepping up to the mic again. If this happens, let the sound person know immediately after the song is over.

Once you've been shocked, you don't ever want it to happen again. For this reason, I carry a foam pop filter/wind screen to every gig. You can pick them up for three or four dollars. Simply slip it over the mic before you start playing, and you won't have to worry about getting shocked (plus, you won't have to worry about who last used the mic).

Feedback/Low Frequency Rumble

Occasionally, you'll get stage feedback or excessive low-end rumble. This is caused by a signal that has looped around on itself. You sing into the mic, and the signal comes out the speaker, right? Well, if a good deal of that signal reaches the microphone again, an endless loop is created. That's when you get that ever-so-pleasant howling sound.

Usually, there's not much you can do about this except inform the soundperson. You might try angling your microphone differently, but this is rarely a permanent fix. Let the soundperson know about it immediately if they can't hear it. (There will be times when the feedback is only coming through the stage monitors and not the main speakers that the audience hears. In these instances, it is possible that the soundperson can't hear the feedback and won't know about it until you tell him.)

CHAPTER 20
MAKING MONEY AS A MUSICIAN: IT CAN BE DONE!

What's Ahead:
- Cover bands
- Private lessons
- High school or college instruction
- Studio musician
- Songwriter
- Other opportunities

You've heard it many times before: *Musicians are always broke.* Utter nonsense! *Pawn shops are filled with music equipment.* Mere coincidence! *You have a better chance of being struck by lightning than you do of "making it" in the music business.* Oh, really? Are these people professional meteorologists or something?

OK, granted, being a musician is probably not the *easiest* way to make a living. If you want job security, you should probably be a teacher, nurse, or some other profession for which there's always a need. However, music *can* be rewarding in other ways than the joy it brings to us, and that includes financial means.

Obviously, there's always the dream of making it, becoming rich and famous, touring the world, and rubbing shoulders with movie stars. And I'm in no way saying that it can't happen. It certainly can and it certainly has for many people over the years. What this chapter deals with, though, is other ways to make ends meet as a musician if this dream happens to elude you.

We'll look at several reliable ways with which musicians have been able to pay the bills and even live quite comfortably. Oftentimes, several of these methods are combined or used to supplement another source of income.

COVER BANDS/WEDDING BANDS

It's a simple fact: people like to hear what they know. If you live anywhere near a fairly metropolitan area, you'd be hard pressed to throw a stone and not hit a bar that hires cover bands. If you're a good cover band and can get people drinking, dancing, and coming back for more, you will get hired. Keep in mind that it's a fairly competitive market, and there are a lot of really good cover bands out there.

Cover bands generally fall into one of two categories: pop and country. A pop cover band's repertoire will usually consist of plenty of dance tunes (from the '60s and '70s up through the present), various pop songs of the day, and perhaps a few novelty songs, as well. Country cover bands usually stick to a country repertoire, although they'll throw in some crossover tunes, as well. Expect to play numerous sets as a cover band. Three or four 45-minute sets are about average. You'll need to have professional, reliable gear and be a rock-steady performer.

Occasionally, pop cover bands break into the wedding circuit, which can be very profitable. It's not uncommon for a four-piece band to make $2,000 or more to play one wedding. Here, the repertoire won't differ much, with the exception of some specific wedding-related songs that you may have to pull off (particularly for a Jewish wedding).

You can start a cover band on your own, but you may have more luck joining an established one. Oftentimes, if you're asked to sub on a gig and you do well, it could turn into a permanent gig. Cover bands often have one or two core members that remain throughout the years as the others come and go as hired guns.

Advantages
- **Steady pay**: Being in a good cover band means a steady paycheck of anywhere from $100 to $1,000 per week (or more in some instances).
- **Fun**: Seeing people dance all night and dig what you're playing is great.
- **High level of musicianship**: You'll get to play with many great musicians in a good cover band, which can be very inspiring.
- **Good contacts**: Oftentimes, players you meet in cover bands can be recruited for other future musical projects. It's also a good way to get friendly with a lot of bar owners and such.

Disadvantages
- **Lack of artistic expression**: People usually want to hear songs like the original, so a cover band doesn't really provide an opportunity for you to say much artistically. If you feel your true calling is to be a songwriter, you might feel a bit hollow in a cover-band situation.
- **Weekends are tied up**: The way cover bands make money is by staying busy. And the busiest times are obviously on the weekends. In this way, being in a cover band is sort of like being a bartender: Your weekends are booked. However, some people get enough enjoyment from playing that they consider it a fair tradeoff. If you really have something important one night, you can usually get a sub. If you get into the habit of doing that, though, your permanent status may get revoked!
- **Monotony**: Playing the same tunes over and over can get a little boring. Many cover bands will try to keep things fresh by working up new hits all the time, but there are certain songs that you're going to have to play over... and over... and over again.

TEACHING PRIVATE LESSONS
Once you feel accomplished enough as a musician, you may consider teaching as a source of income. It's a fairly reliable way to generate a good supplemental income as a musician, and many people make a very good living at it. There are a number of avenues you could go down when considering the teaching route.

School affiliation: Oftentimes, local colleges (especially community colleges) provide a teaching opportunity. This can be either a salaried position or a rate based on how many students you teach.

Music store: Music stores are a possibility, as well. Many stores allow you to "rent" a studio space and teach out of their store. They usually take a portion of your hourly rate as payment. This can be anywhere from 25 to 50 percent. It may seem excessive, but it's usually easier to get students when you've got the clout of a music store behind you.

Private: Private instructors often teach out of their home or studio. Some private instructors will make house calls for certain students, although this is less common.

Teaching privately on your own usually requires more advertising than the other methods. Most instructors run ads in the local classifieds, hang flyers in supermarkets and/or music stores, and place ads on the internet. Oftentimes, instructors will develop a large student base with one of the above methods (school or music store) and then take those students with them when they decide to go private.

Advantages

- **Be your own boss**: If you have enough students to support yourself without another source of income, you're the boss. You get all of the freedoms that affords.
- **Profitable**: Music instructors usually earn anywhere from $20 to $60 an hour or more for private lessons. If you don't have to pay rent for a teaching studio at a music store, this is not a bad wage. And if you're able to maintain a full-time load of students, you can, indeed, make a very comfortable living.
- **Job security**: Once you've developed a full-time student base, there's usually a fairly inflexible demand for music teachers. If you're willing to teach children, your potential to earn money will greatly increase.
- **Sense of achievement**: It's a great feeling when you encounter a student who really excels and goes on to great things.

Disadvantages

- **Monotony**: Though exceptional students do exist, you'll run into a good amount who are simply there because of their parents. Their lack of interest can get a little old.
- **Difficult to start**: It's difficult to start from ground zero and build up a full load of students. It requires a fair amount of self promotion, and if this doesn't sound like you, then perhaps you might want to try the other previously mentioned methods.
- **Lack of artistic expression**: You're probably not going to feel incredibly inspired by showing students the major scale over and over. This is why many private instructors also belong to bands or pursue other musical endeavors.

TEACHING HIGH SCHOOL OR COLLEGE MUSIC

For someone who wants to be involved in or around music, but doesn't want to worry about where the next meal is coming from, teaching at a high school or college may be the way to go. Obviously, this will almost always require a good deal of education and usually a bachelor's degree (or perhaps more for the college level), but that's a fair investment if you want to make a lifelong career out of it. For those with a love for classical and choral music, a teaching career may be the way to go.

Advantages

- **Steady pay and job security**: Teaching music in a school is perhaps the most regular job you can have when it comes to using your music skills.
- **Summers off**: This one can be quite appealing for many.
- **Sense of achievement**: You'll have the opportunity to really inspire people and make a difference in their lives.

Disadvantages

- **Initial investment**: You must go to college and earn a degree before you're allowed to mold young minds.
- **Politics**: At times, you may be dealing with grumpy parents, grumpy administrators, or both.
- **Lack of artistic expression**: This seems to be a recurring theme. Some music teachers claim to be fulfilled with their job, but others choose to express themselves through additional musical means.

STUDIO MUSICIANS

Studio musician. The mere term has reached nearly holy-grail status among the commoners. Studio musicians are professional musicians who are hired to perform on recordings, commercial jingles, etc. It's a very tough business to break into, but once you've got your foot in the door and start making a name for yourself, it can be very lucrative.

Although most of the big-time work lies in the major musical hotbeds like Los Angeles, Nashville, and New York, there are still numerous opportunities in most large cities such as Dallas, Chicago, and Seattle, among others. Local companies often hire studio musicians to play on their commercials, and sometimes songwriters pay studio musicians to play on demos. This can provide a great opportunity for supplemental income. However, if you really want to make the big bucks as a studio musician, you'll need to relocate to a major metropolis.

Studio musicians are some of the highest caliber musicians around. You need good music-reading ability, great chops, topnotch professional equipment (and the knowledge it takes to get great sounds from it), a command of many different styles, and great networking ability.

Advantages

- **High earning potential**: If you really break into the studio-musician world, you're going to be living the life of luxury. It's very tough to do, and the competition is fierce, but it can be done.
- **Exciting and dynamic work**: The life of a studio musician can be fast-paced and can result in rubbing shoulders with some huge names in the music business.
- **Excellent contacts**: You'll meet all kinds of stars and bigwigs, and these contacts could lead to many more opportunities down the road.

Disadvantages

- **Stiff competition**: It's been said that Nashville has some of the best musicians you'll ever hear, and those are just the ones sweeping up after the professional musicians! In the professional music world, time is money, and if and when you're hired for your first job, you want to get it right in as few takes as possible.
- **Unpredictable schedule**: As a studio musician, especially in the big leagues, you'll need to be available on almost an on-call basis. If you get a call for a gig and aren't available, rest assured there's a long line of players ready to step in.
- **Erratic/unsteady income**: Until you're well established, it can be feast or famine. Many studio musicians are forced to keep other part-time jobs to make ends meet.

PROFESSIONAL SONGWRITERS

Another holy-grail profession among musicians, *professional songwriters* write songs that are recorded by major artists. Nowadays, there are plenty of artists who write their own music, but in the old days, this wasn't the norm. Buddy Holly, the Beatles, and other early pioneers started the artist/writer total-package trend in the '50s and '60s that has continued to gain steam to this day.

Today, by far the largest market for the professional songwriter lies in country music. It's the last genre that still possesses a fairly distinct line between writers and performers. However, more and more "young country" artists, such as Toby Keith and Shania Twain, are writing more and more of their material. So it's hard to tell how much longer the songwriter market will remain open in the country world. There are still opportunities for songwriters in other genres, but compared to country, they're few and far between.

If you think you'd like to give it a go as a songwriter, there are tons of reference materials out there. Books upon books have been written to aid the struggling songwriter, and there are also plenty of books that help put you in touch with publishers, co-writers, etc.

Advantages

- **Artistic expression**: Finally! Yes, you'll get to express yourself as a songwriter, even if it's not necessarily your chosen genre. Some people who have a knack for writing really catchy songs stumbled into writing country songs, even though they aren't fans of the genre.
- **Flexible schedule**: Write when you want, where you want. Although you'll obviously need to do something else to pay the rent until you have that first hit.
- **Contacts**: You can meet plenty of important people as a songwriter and earn their respect and admiration. Many famous performers, such as Willie Nelson and Barry Manilow, started out as songwriters and crossed over.
- **Huge-income potential**: If you write a few songs that become Top 10 hits and stay there for a while, you'll most likely be set for life if you're not careless with your money. Of course, there are many shades of gray between nothing and "set for life," and there are those who simply make a comfortable living without ever having written a Top 10 or even Top 40 hit.

Disadvantages

- **Stiff competition**: As with the world of studio musicians, there are thousands and thousands of songwriters trying to hit the jackpot. But that's only an obstacle if you consider it one. Many have made it, so it can certainly be done.
- **Lack of steady pay**: You could try your hand at writing songs for 20 years and not make a dime from it. It's possible. It's also possible (although unlikely) that your fifth song could become a hit. Needless to say, unless you're living off a large inheritance, you're going to have to support yourself by other means until things start happening.
- **Rejection**: You may hear "no thanks" many times before you strike gold. If you don't handle rejection well, it may not be the way to go.

OTHER OPPORTUNITIES

In addition to the aforementioned prospects, there are plenty of other ways to fill your pockets via your musical skills. Here are just a few:

Film Scorer

This is another area that's a bit tough to break into, but it can be very rewarding, as well as extremely lucrative. If you're interested in this, try scoring a few student films pro bono to see if it suits your fancy. Everything you do can be stored in your portfolio, and an impressive portfolio can possibly get you a shot at a paying gig.

Sound Engineer

You can work in a recording studio or in live sound as an engineer. If you enjoy playing with musical toys, pushing buttons, and plugging in cables, this is the job for you. There are many trade schools dedicated to this type of training, or you can get a pretty good education by studying on your own. Plus, you can gain good experience by frequently volunteering your services (running sound for your friend's band, church, etc.).

Transcriber/Music Engraver

You know all those tab books you see at the music store? Well, someone had to transcribe those songs, and someone had to engrave the music. Music-publishing companies often hire freelance transcribers and engravers for these projects. You can contact the company, and if they're hiring they'll have you submit examples of your work and prove your abilities through an "audition."

Freelance Writer/Editor

Magazines, publishers, and websites often hire freelance writers or editors for help with articles on various musical topics. You can directly contact the magazine or site to see if they have work. If so, they'll have you submit examples of your work and perhaps give you an evaluative assignment.

All About Gear

CHAPTER 21

THE BASS AND AMPLIFIER: A MATCH MADE IN HEAVEN

What's Ahead:
- Choosing a bass
- Choosing an amplifier
- Buying used or new

My first instrument (a guitar) was borrowed from a friend of mine who no longer played it. It wasn't exactly the "crème de la crème," and my parents refused to buy me my own until I proved it wasn't another hobby that would end up in the corner of my closet after a month. If you went through a similar rite of passage, you know what it feels to want your first *real* instrument. You've come to the right chapter. Here we're going to explore the many options available to you in the realm of basses and amplifiers, discuss how to get exactly what you're looking for, and alert you to some pitfalls to watch out for.

I just remembered something: My parents didn't actually buy my first instrument. I bought it with money I saved up from working at a supermarket. They did spring for lessons, though, so I guess that makes it all right.

OPTION ANXIETY: SO MANY BASSES!

Purchasing your first bass is a bit daunting. The number of basses on the market is quite staggering, to say the least, and it's very easy to get overwhelmed. If you go into a music store without thinking ahead in terms of what you want, you could end up walking out with way more bass than you need or really want. To avoid this, simply take the time to identify your core needs in a bass before you hand over your cash. You might start by answering the following questions:

What style of music do I want to play? Most basses are capable of handling a wide range of styles; you can easily use the same bass for your basic rock, country, blues, and jazz gigs. However, certain styles are best handled with a specific bass. For instance, many nü-metal bands prefer to play very low, heavy riffs. Therefore, five-string basses are quite popular because of the added low range.

How much do I want to spend? As with buying a car, you can get fast-talked into buying something you don't really want if you're not careful. Those people working at the music store are working on commission! If you don't fall under the "money is no object" category, decide on a budget before you try out your first bass. You can spend anywhere from $100 to $5,000 or more on a bass.

Are you in it for the long haul? If you're unsure as to whether or not the bass is going to be a lifelong passion, you should probably just get your feet wet before diving in headlong. There are a number of beginner basses on the market that can sound quite good, and they can end up functioning as a back-up instrument should you outgrow them.

What type of electronics do you need? Are you going to need a great deal of tonal variety, or is one humbucking pickup going to suffice? The more electronic options the bass features, the greater the tonal variety you will have at your disposal. However, more complicated is not always better. If you're the type who gets easily overwhelmed by too many options, perhaps you'd be better off keeping it simple.

By answering some simple questions such as these, you can eliminate many options right away.

Fender: The Standard, for Good Reason

If you've assessed your needs and have decided that you want to get a good bass that you can use throughout your career, you really can't go wrong with a Fender Precision or a Fender Jazz. The Precision ("P" bass) has been used on more recordings than any bass in history, and the Jazz bass is extremely popular, as well.

Besides the difference in body shape, the two basses feature different pickup configurations, which results in noticeably different tones. The P-bass has one humbucking pickup, while the Jazz bass has two single coils. It's been said that the P-bass "thumps," while the Jazz bass "growls."

The American-made versions of these basses are the top of the heap, and you can get a new one for around $1,000. There are many other import models offered that can be had for much cheaper. Though the quality is not as high as in the American models (which are pretty much the industry standard), they make fine beginner/ intermediate basses and will do nicely as a back-up bass if you're in a bind.

Jazz bass

Precision bass

Other Notable Mentions

While there are several truly original bass designs, the many available basses are basically other company's versions of the popular Precision-bass and Jazz-bass designs. Here are some big players in the bass arena:

Sadowsky

Sadowsky produces several higher-end versions of the Jazz-bass format, although they do have a few P-bass-style basses, as well. Expect to pay at least $2,000 for a new Sadowsky.

Lakland

Pronounced "lakeland," this company produces not only numerous versions of the Jazz and P-bass, but also many of their own unique designs. They have models starting at around $700 new and on up.

Music Man

Leo Fender (yes, *that* Fender) started the Music Man bass line, which is manufactured by Ernie Ball, in the early '80s. They've grown in popularity throughout the years, and their "Stingray" model is among the most popular of all basses today. They can be had for a little over $1,000.

Rickenbacker

Rickenbackers became very popular in the '70s and have remained a favorite to this day. They feature a cool, vintage look and a unique tone that can be heard on the Beatles' *Revolver* album, among others.

Hofner

Also popularized by the Beatles' Paul McCartney, the Hofner is the famous violin-shaped bass. The 500/1 model, now known as the "Beatle bass," features a unique semi-acoustic design and a warm, woody tone.

Alembic

In 1951, Fender's Precision bass was certainly the biggest event in the electric bass's history. Alembic's creation of the ultra–high end bass in 1971, featuring active electronics, fine woods, and neck-thru construction, is certainly a fine candidate for the second biggest.

There are plenty of other bass manufacturers, including Peavey, Ibanez, Warwick, Fodera (the first 6-string model), Carvin, and Spector, that make fine instruments, as well. Whatever your needs, chances are there's a bass out there to match.

Other Aspects to Consider

Here are some more things to keep in mind when choosing a bass:

Electronics: Active or Passive?

There are two types of electronic configurations available on electric basses: *active* or *passive*. The short of it is that active electronics require a 9-volt battery to work, while passive pickups require no battery at all.

Active pickups (with a fresh battery) provide a hotter output signal than passive, and the sound is usually easier to tweak and control with EQ than with passive pickups. The battery is usually activated when the cable is plugged into your bass, so if you choose an active bass you'll need to get into the habit of unplugging your bass or you'll be changing batteries a lot! (Changing batteries can be a bit of a pain, too, because it usually requires you to unscrew a plate on the back of the bass.)

Feel vs. Sound vs. Look

It's easy to try to hear with our eyes, and sometimes we think we have our mind made up on an instrument without ever having played it or heard it. It just looks so cool! However, this is not grounds for purchase, unless you're just planning to display it on your wall. If that perfect-looking instrument doesn't feel or sound right to you, then it's not right. Period. You're going to be spending a lot of time with this instrument, and the way it feels and sounds is going to stick with you more than its looks. If you're willing to look hard enough, you'll probably find a bass that has all three.

Don't Buy the First Bass You Touch

If you haven't shopped around much for a new bass, it's easy to fall under the "all that glitters is gold" spell. Any shiny new bass in your hands can feel like a million dollars if you're used to playing a hand-me-down. You could end up making an impulse purchase only to later realize that the bass isn't what you really want. There's a very simple rule that you can follow to avoid this predicament: Play at least ten different basses before you decide on one. It may very well be that the first bass you played turns out to be "the one," but exposing yourself to the many other options available first helps to make sure of that.

Don't Buy an Instrument You Haven't Played Unless...

The only time you should consider buying an instrument you haven't played is if it's offered with some type of money-back guarantee. An instrument could look to be in perfect shape in many photos from all different angles, but it could still have a number of problems that can be costly to repair. A simple five-minute test with most basses can clear up any preconceived notions you may have, but if you purchase something with no guarantee, only to find out later that something's wrong, you may end up eating the cost of the repairs.

Many catalogs, such as *Musician's Friend* and *Sweetwater*, will offer 30-day satisfaction guarantees on most instruments sold, but if you buy from eBay or some other online source, you need to be very careful of the fine print.

THE AMPLIFIER: YOUR BASS'S LOUDMOUTH FRIEND

Unlike acoustic instruments, electric basses are barely audible when they're unplugged. Even when they are plugged in, the signal generated is very low and needs to be significantly raised before it reaches a level with which any serious damage can be done. This is where the *amplifier*, or "amp," comes in. The amplifier takes the signal from your bass, boosts it to an audible level, and then sends it to the *speaker*, where it's broadcasted for all to hear. If one of these elements is missing, you won't be able to vibrate or rattle anything.

To Combine or Not—That Is the Question

Amplifiers are available in two basic formats: a *separate amp and speaker*, or a *combo amp*.

Separate amp and speaker: In this configuration, the amp is cased in its own housing and the speaker in a separate "speaker cabinet." A speaker cable is used to connect the two. Although they're often sold as a pair, you have the freedom of using the amp (known as the "head") with any suitable speaker cabinet, thus allowing you to test several different speaker/amp combinations. Different speakers do sound quite different, so this is a nice option to have.

Speaker cables are not the same as instrument cables, although they look the same and have the same 1/4" plug at the end. (Don't let a music store salesperson tell you differently, because some will.) Using an instrument cable instead of a speaker cable could damage your equipment, so use caution.

Combo amp: A combo amp is simply an amp head and speaker contained within the same box. The main advantage this setup has is portability, as it's easier to haul around one box than two. On the downside, you're stuck with that speaker when you purchase the amp.

It is possible to use a separate speaker enclosure with a combo amp by running a speaker cable from the "speaker out" jack to a separate speaker cabinet. By doing this, you'll be using the separate speaker cabinet instead of the speaker inside your combo amp. Some players do this if they really like the speaker in their combo amp but occasionally want the tone of a different speaker.

Combo amps make great starter amps, and they can sound great, too. They're easy to cart from the practice room to the rehearsal and gig, and they're less of a hassle. The prices range from about $200 or so on up (and up!). The separate amp and speaker configurations usually start a bit higher—around $400 or so. The separate amp and speaker setup is used more in the professional world.

Speakers: Is Bigger Always Better?

Bass-amp speakers come in various sizes, though the most common are 10" and 15". The general rule of thumb is this: larger speakers produce more bass response (and, therefore, more "boominess"), and smaller speakers produce less bass response (and, therefore, a clearer, punchier tone). Before you buy an amp (combo or separate), experiment with different speaker sizes to hear what sound suits your fancy. You may end up with several different speaker cabinets, using different ones for different types of gigs.

Tube vs. Solid-state

In the early days, all amplifiers made use of *vacuum tube technology*, similar to old televisions and radios. However, since the '70s, amps have been widely available with solid-state technology as well, which relies on the use of *transistors* instead of tubes.

"Tube" amps sound slightly different than solid-state amps; however, it's a matter of personal preference as to which one you choose. If you're more practical, you might opt for solid-state, as tubes wear out and need to be replaced periodically. However, many people swear that solid-state amps can't compete with a tube-amp's tone. If you're not put off by a bit of maintenance and a slightly higher price tag, you may turn into a tube-amp player.

Vacuum tubes

Some Standards in the Amp World

Amplifiers, just like basses, come in all shapes, sizes, and colors. Here are a few of the more popular models that will get most jobs done. Remember that your ears should be the final judge! No amount of specs can compare with sitting down in front of an amp to hear what it can do. When you're trying out amps, use your bass (if you already have one). Using a bass other than your own to try out an amp is like a man trying on clothes for his wife—it's just wrong!

Ampeg SVT

SWR SM-500

Gallien-Krueger Microbass

Mesa Boogie Bass 400+

USED OR NEW?

When buying a bass, amp, or pretty much any musical equipment, we musicians have a choice. Just about every single piece of gear you can find new can usually be found used, at a discounted price. Sometimes this discount is negligible, but occasionally it reaches 50 percent or more! Some huge bargains can be found by going the used-gear route, but you can also get burned if you're not careful.

Always make sure you understand all the fine print when buying used. Look out for phrases like:
- "All sales final."
- "No returns or exchanges."
- "No refunds available."
- "No guarantee or warranty."

If you see anything like this, I suggest moving on, no matter how good the deal may seem. There are plenty of used items that carry some sort of a guarantee (even if it's only guaranteed not to be D.O.A.), and the few extra dollars you may pay is well worth the piece of mind.

Money-back Guarantees and Restocking Fees

New gear will often come with a 30- or 45-day money-back guarantee, but you still need to read the fine print. Some stores charge a "restocking fee" when you return an item for a refund. (This is done to avoid people treating the guarantee as a free gear rental, which is understandable.) They're sneaky about this, too. Many times you'll make a purchase, decide you don't like it, and return it. When you say you didn't know about the restocking-fee policy, they'll say, "Well, it's printed on your receipt!" This may be true, but you didn't receive the receipt, of course, until *after* you made the purchase! If you ever do consider making a purchase with the money-back guarantee in mind, be sure to ask the salesperson about any such fees beforehand.

CHAPTER 22
ACCESSORIZE! EFFECTS, TOOLS, AND OTHER IMPORTANT KNICK-KNACKS

What's Ahead:
- The absolute essential equipment, besides the bass and amp
- Other recommended items
- Effects pedals

Besides the bass and amp, there are still plenty of other items you'll need to keep your bass-playing operation running smoothly. Some of these are absolutely essential, while others are a matter of preference (and some matters of preference may end up becoming essential to you). Of course, your bass deserves the best, so why not treat it that way?

THE BAREBONES ESSENTIALS

If you've got a bass, amp, and the items below, you're at least up and running. But you don't want to do the bare minimum, do you? (See Chapter 1 for more photos.)

- **Case or gig bag**: You can't carry your bass around by holding it in your hands. It's bound to get bumped, scratched, and who knows what else? For ultimate protection, a hardshell case is the way to go, but a soft gig bag (usually made of nylon or leather) with a shoulder strap is also a convenient option if you're frequently on the go.

- **Strap**: If you're going to be standing up at all, you've got to have a strap. Even if you're not standing, a strap is nice because it allows you to use your hands for other various tasks without having to set your bass down.

- **Cable**: This is pretty obvious, but you'll be surprised by how many times people end up borrowing a cable from someone else.

- **Strings**: Ideally, you should always have several extra sets in your possession, but you need to have at least one extra set. You can usually save a few dollars by buying them in packs of ten or 12.

- **Picks**: If you use them, keep a bunch on hand at all times. They have a tendency to fall through the cracks and end up in a parallel universe if you drop them.

If you have trouble with losing picks, try to get into the habit of sticking it between the strings near the first fret when you're done playing. This way, you should always have a pick available when you pick up your bass.

HIGHLY RECOMMENDED ITEMS

Here are the next things to start adding to your arsenal as soon as you acquire the aforementioned essentials:

- **Electronic tuner**: Learning to tune by ear is important (see Chapter 3), but if you plan on playing with other musicians (which you should) you need a tuner. Tuners come in a variety of shapes and sizes. Some are designed to sit on a desktop (which usually translates to your knee), while others are rack-mountable. Another common design, especially for players who gig often, is the foot-pedal tuner. This allows you to run your signal through the pedal to your amp. When you depress the pedal, it's activated and your signal is muted while you check your tuning.

- **Bass stand**: There are few things more frustrating than needing to set your bass down and having no good place to do it. A stand is invaluable for times like this. Many models of stands fold into a very manageable size for easy transportation. These types are great for taking to the gig.

- **Metronome**: Practice playing with this little guy, and your band members will thank you. As part of the rhythm section, our sense of time is extremely important, and there's no better way to develop it. Playing along with albums works well, too, but if you're practicing something on your own, always use a metronome, if possible.

- **Tools**: It helps to keep a set of various tools with your bass should you need to make any slight adjustments or repairs (see Chapter 24). This could include screw drivers, Allen wrenches, pliers, wire cutters, etc.

- **Music stand**: A music stand holds your music so you don't have to balance it on your knees or squint to read it off the ground.

- **Cleaning supplies**: If you want to keep your bass looking new and shiny, it helps to have the right tools. These include a plain cotton cloth, guitar polish (not furniture polish!), fretboard oil, polishing/jewelry cloth, and rubbing alcohol.

SEASON TO TASTE: EFFECT PEDALS

Beyond the previously mentioned items, we still have the realm of effects to consider. These can shape your sound in many different ways, both in subtle and extreme fashion. Take a weekend afternoon or two and head down to the music store to try out some of these and see what you think.

- **Volume pedal**: This isn't an effect, per se, but it falls in the same category. This pedal allows you to control the volume of your bass with your foot instead of the volume knob. When in the fully up position, no signal passes through the pedal. When the pedal is fully pressed down, your signal passes through unaffected. This can be a very handy device to create volume swells or to simply give you a boost at a certain point in the song for dramatic effect.

- **Chorus pedal**: A chorus pedal makes it sound as though there is more than one bass playing. It does this by slowly detuning and retuning the signal, producing anywhere from a slight doubling effect to an underwater warbling effect.

- **Delay pedal**: A delay pedal (or echo pedal) creates one or more echoes of everything you play. This can be used as a subtle device, or the echoes can be set to fall in between the notes you play to create a rhythmically complex texture.

- **Flanger or phase shifter**: These pedals create a sort of swooshing sound that was popular in the '60s and '70s.

- **Distortion/fuzz**: A distortion pedal imitates the sound of a tube amp distorting or "breaking up." The sound is thick and dirty and can be used to fatten up a line. Guitar players use distortion quite often.

- **Octave pedal**: An octave pedal will double your lines at either an octave above or below what you're playing (or both).

SECTION **9**

Care and Maintenance

CHAPTER 23
CHANGING STRINGS:
YOUR BASS GUITAR'S OUTPATIENT SURGERY

What's Ahead:
- Determining the time to make the change
- Removing the old strings
- Putting new strings on
- Tips on how to improve string life

If you've had your bass for a while, and it doesn't seem to sound as lively as it once did, don't panic. It's just time for your first bit of maintenance; it's time to change the strings. This is a minor procedure that's perfectly safe and can be completed on an outpatient basis (meaning you don't need to take it to the repair shop, unless you want to waste $15).

WHEN IS IT TIME TO CHANGE?

Since the life of your strings depends on several things, including how often you play, how much you sweat, and how often you clean the strings, there's no one set length of time to wait before changing them. However, there are several indicators that let you know they're ready to go.

- **Visible markings**: As your strings get older, you'll see spots and discoloration along them. They won't be bright and shiny anymore.

- **Dull sound**: New strings have plenty of life in their sound. When strings get old, they begin to sound dull and muddy and lack clarity or brightness. They also won't sustain notes for as long; the pitches will decay sooner.

- **Difficulty in tuning**: Harmonics aren't as clear in old strings, making it harder to tune.

- **Strings feel rusty or sticky**: This is a definitive sign that they need to go. They needed to go a while ago, actually.

BEGINNING THE OPERATION: TAKING OFF THE OLD STRINGS

First thing's first. Before you start hacking away, make sure you have a full set of new strings! I know it sounds obvious, but how many times have you been stuck in the restroom without any tissue paper?

There's not much to taking off the strings. The easiest and quickest way is to use a wire cutter. Detune all the strings to the point of slack and simply snip them off. Unwind the top portion from the tuning pegs and pull the other halves (with the ball-end) back through the bridge.

danger

Don't forget to detune the strings before you cut them, unless you want to risk getting smacked across the face with one of them! There's a great deal of tension in a tuned string, and if you cut it with all that tension intact, look out!

Sterilizing the Patient (Cleaning the Fretboard)

Before you put on new strings, make sure you clean the frets and fretboard as discussed in Chapter 24. After this is done and the appropriate amount of anesthetic has been administered, you may proceed with the operation.

MAKING THE TRANSPLANT: ATTACHING NEW STRINGS

New strings are individually coiled and are usually numbered or color-coded to let you know which one goes where. The higher the number of the string gauge, the thicker the string is (and, therefore, lower in pitch). Your fourth string will have the highest number, and the first string will have the lowest number.

Some people prefer to place the bass on their lap (don't sit in a chair with arm rests), while others place the bass on a table. Others choose to place the bass on the floor. Whichever method you choose, make sure there's no danger of it falling. (I advise against stringing in your lap unless you're over a carpeted floor.)

- Carefully uncoil the string (it can poke you if you're not careful!) and thread the pointed end through the appropriate hole in the bridge. Pull the string through until the ball end hits the bridge.

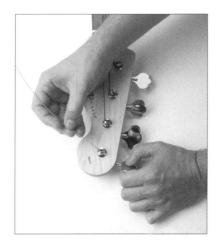

- Now thread the pointed end through the appropriate tuning-peg hole. Pull it tight and then bend it so that the string rests into the groove.

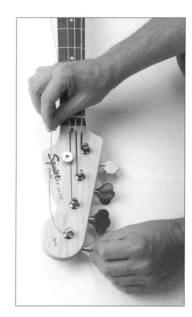

- While holding the string with one hand, wind the tuning peg with the other to gradually increase the tension on the string.

- When the string begins to tighten up past the point of slack, check to make sure it's sitting in the appropriate bridge saddle.

- Repeat this process for each string.

After all the strings are on, begin tuning them up, checking the pitch with your tuner. The strings will need to be tuned several times before they will hold to pitch. This can be helped along by periodically stretching the strings out while tuning them.

POST-OPERATIVE PROCEDURES: HOW TO KEEP YOUR NEW STRINGS HEALTHY

New bass strings cost anywhere from $12 to $40 a set, so unless you're made of money, you'll want to get the most life out of them as possible. (Even if you're made of money, you'd probably rather be playing your bass than restringing it. If not, then you're in the wrong field. You should be a bass-guitar tech, not a bass guitarist!) In order to ensure the longest life possible for your strings, be sure to follow these doctor's orders:

- **Always, always, always wash your hands before you play**: Dirt and oils from your hands are string killers. In some instances, washing your hands alone can extend the life of your strings by months. Different players have different luck with this. I once knew a guy who *said* he washed his hands all the time before playing his bass, but his strings were disgusting after about a week. (I think he was lying, though.)

- **Clean your strings regularly**: Make it a habit of cleaning your strings weekly, at least. See Chapter 24 for details.

- **When possible, keep the bass in its case**: Keeping it locked up will prolong the life of your strings and reduce the risk of any other type of damage caused by running children, pets, etc.

CHAPTER 24

A CLEAN, LEAN MACHINE: HELP YOUR BASS LOOK AND PERFORM ITS BEST

What's Ahead:
- Cleaning and polishing
- Adjusting the intonation and action
- Electric problems
- Proper storage of your bass

Your bass is your baby, and you want it to stay innocent and out of harm's way, right? Well, regardless of your best efforts, it's more than likely that your instrument will get a few bruises at some point. But we can do everything in our power to minimize and prevent them. Cleaning our bass regularly can help reduce the appearance of fine lines and wrinkles and ensure healthy looking skin for years to come (skin on the bass, that is; not your skin—you're on your own with that).

Besides a good cleaning, we need to keep our instrument at the top of its game performance-wise, as well. In this chapter, we'll look at several important tweaks that can be done to help our bass stay fit and healthy.

CLEANING

There are many different parts to the bass, and each one requires special attention when cleaning. Some parts may go months without need for cleaning, while others could use it every time you set the instrument down.

The Neck and Body

For these parts you'll use a cotton cloth (a T-shirt works nicely—an old T-shirt that is!) and some guitar polish, which is available at most music stores. Work some into the cloth and rub down the body and the back of the neck (not the fretboard). Your bass will shine like new—and smell polish-y, too!

The Fretboard and Frets

The following should be done when you change strings, after the old strings have been taken off. For the frets, use a polishing cloth; these are often used for jewelry cleaning and already have polish applied to them. Buff the frets with a cotton cloth, and look away, lest you go blind by the shine!

After wiping free the visible dirt with a plain cotton cloth, the fretboard should be cleaned with a cloth and some fingerboard oil. Not much oil is needed; a few drops on the cloth should be enough.

The Strings

You can always give the strings a good wipe-down after each playing session, but if you really want to help extend their life, use some rubbing alcohol. After allowing a cloth to absorb the alcohol for a few seconds, simply pinch a string with the cloth and run up and down the length of the string.

The Pickups and Hardware

The hardware (the bridge, knobs, tuning pegs, etc.) can usually be kept looking shiny and new by buffing them with a cotton cloth every now and then. If needed, you can use a minimum strength brass or metal polish, but be sure to avoid the wood.

The pickups should only be cleaned with a cloth or cotton swab (to help get to the cracks between the pickups and pickguard or wood). Don't use any fluids when cleaning the pickups, or you could damage them.

MAKING NECESSARY ADJUSTMENTS

Bass guitars are delicate instruments with many delicate parts, and sometimes these parts need a slight adjustment. Some of these adjustments are made to suit personal taste, while others need to be done to help the instrument perform properly.

Setting the Intonation

Having your bass properly intonated will allow you to play all over the neck without going out of tune. Here's a quick test that you can perform to hear if your bass's intonation needs adjusting:

Play an octave shape on fret 1 and 3, using both your 4/2 string group and your 3/1 string group. (In other words, you should be playing octave F notes and octave B♭ notes.) Make sure these octaves are in tune.

Now play those same shapes an octave higher on the fretboard, at fret 13. If these octaves are out of tune, your bass needs to be intonated. Here's the procedure:

- Play a harmonic at fret 12, and tune the string with a tuner.
- Now play the twelfth fret normally, and check the tuning against the tuner.
- **If the fretted note is flat compared to the harmonic**:

    At the back of the bridge, loosen the appropriate screw for the string that you're intonating. This will decrease the length of the string. Repeat this process, checking the tuning of the fretted twelfth fret against the twelfth-fret harmonic, until the pitches are the same.

- **If the fretted note is sharp compared to the harmonic**:

    At the back of the bridge, tighten the appropriate screw for the string you're intonating. This will increase the length of the string. Repeat this process, checking the tuning of the fretted twelfth fret against the twelfth-fret harmonic, until the pitches are the same.

- Repeat the above process for each string.

Setting the Action

You don't have to be a daredevil for your bass to have great *action*. The action on your bass is the space between your strings and the fretboard. The higher the strings are off the fretboard, the higher the action is. The action can be adjusted two ways: using the *trussrod* or the *bridge saddles*.

Adjusting the Truss Rod

The truss rod adjusts the relief of the neck. The *relief* is the slight curvature that's needed to allow the strings to vibrate freely. If the neck was perfectly flat with no relief, the strings would constantly rattle against the frets. If the relief is too great, the action will be so high that the bass will become very difficult to play. A happy middle ground is what's desired.

Here's a test that you can use to check the action. Press down on the first fret of the low E string with your left hand, and press down on the last fret of the same string with your right hand. While you're holding both of these frets down, look at the space between the low E string and the twelfth fret. It should be about the width of a business card or so. If it's much higher or lower than that, you probably need to adjust the truss rod.

You should have received an Allen wrench with your bass. This is used to adjust the truss rod. (If you don't have an Allen wrench, you can find one at your local music store.) The truss rod is adjusted either at the headstock or at the neck/body joint.

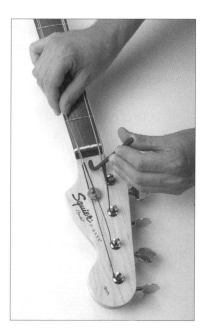

If the action is too high, tighten the trussrod by turning the wrench clockwise.

If the action is too low, loosen the trussrod by turning the wrench counter-clockwise.

Do not turn the wrench farther than one quarter turn at a time when adjusting the truss rod. You need to allow time for the wood to resettle. If you force the trussrod too quickly, you could crack the neck.

Adjusting the Height of the Bridge Saddles

The action can also be raised and lowered on a string-by-string basis using the bridge saddles. Using the tiny Allen wrench provided with your bass (again, contact your local music store if you don't have one), you can raise or lower the individual strings by adjusting these screws on the bridge saddles.

If you're afraid of improperly setting your action, you might consider having your guitar "set up" by a professional repair person. This will include setting the intonation, action, and a few other minor adjustments, and will cost about $50–$60. At that point, you can see (or feel) what a proper set up feels like.

The Final Adjustment to Your Bass's Playability: Your Fingernails!

You can have your bass set up like a dream by the finest repair man this side of the Atlantic, but it's not going to amount to a hill of beans if you don't tend to your own affairs. As a bass player, long fingernails are not your friend—on either hand!

On the left hand, they get in the way of proper fretting technique, resulting in some players bending back their first finger joint. This is a big no-no and could lead to injury. Long nails on the right hand result in the nail making contact with the string when plucking, which results in a thin tone. Classical guitarists make use of their nails for plucking, but it doesn't work on bass.

Do yourself (and your bass) a favor: keep those nails trimmed!

ELECTRICAL ISSUES

Occasionally, you may run into problems with your bass's electronics (pickups, knobs, etc.). These sorts of problems usually require opening up the bass to get a look "under the hood." It could be that a pickup has gone bad, a solder connection has come loose, or any number of things. If you're handy with this type of thing and have a DIY spirit, there are plenty of books on the subject of guitar and bass repair. If you'd rather not venture into that sort of territory, then it's off to the repair shop. Repairs can get a bit costly, however. You probably won't get out of there without spending $40–$50. So, if you're up to it, learning how to change pickups or other components is worth it, in my opinion.

KEEPING YOUR BASS SAFE AND SOUND: PROPER STORAGE

Let's get this out of the way right now: "Proper storage" does not mean placing the bass down face-first on your bed. If you're leaving your bass for an hour or so, you can leave it on its stand. However, if you won't be playing for a day or two, put the bass in its case. Besides protecting it from sunlight exposure and other elements, it keeps it nearly 100-percent safe from harm. That is, unless something huge, like a meteor or jet engine, falls on your house. But then, your damaged bass probably isn't your biggest concern.

When possible, basses and guitars should be stored in a climate-controlled environment. Don't leave them (even inside the case) in a cold basement or garage, a hot attic, or in the hot trunk of a car. Just use common sense, really. Don't leave your bass anywhere you wouldn't want it to leave you. In other words, do unto your bass as you'd have it do unto you.

Who's Who

CHAPTER 25
TEN PLAYERS WHO CHANGED THE WORLD OF BASS

What's Ahead:
- Ten influential players and how they changed the bass

Here are a few heavy hitters in the world of the electric bass guitar who redefined the boundaries of the instrument in one way or another. This list is hardly comprehensive and is growing continually; however, these players are certainly a good start.

JAMES JAMERSON

Jamerson is the electric bass's first true virtuoso. As the fore-most bassist for the Funk Brothers (the Motown label's famous rhythm section), he played on more hits than you can shake a stick at, including "What's Going On" (Marvin Gaye), "Dancing in the Streets" (Martha & the Vandellas), and "For Once in My Life" (Stevie Wonder), among many, many more. His daring and melodic approach completely redefined the instrument's role in pop music, and his influence is felt immensely to this day.

Photo provided by Frank Driggs Collection

Photo by Richard Aaron

PAUL McCARTNEY

It's hard to believe that a bass player as influential and famous as McCartney only took to the instrument because no one else in his band wanted to play it. Of course, that band was the most famous pop band in music history. McCartney's incredibly melodic bass lines, epitomized on Beatles classics such as "Something," "Paperback Writer," and countless others, brought the bass to the foreground in a vocal- and guitar-dominated genre.

JACO PASTORIUS

Jaco (as he was known) was unanimously viewed as the world's greatest bass player during his prime, in the '70s and early '80s. His virtuosity on the fretless bass was absolutely unprecedented, and his accomplishments as a composer and arranger were equally impressive. His busy but fluent grooves and effortless, horn-like leads have inspired legions of followers. Besides his brilliant solo work and countless session appearances, he was also a prominent member of the fusion supergroup Weather Report, along with legends Joe Zawinul and Wayne Shorter. "Donna Lee" and "Come On, Come Over" are essential.

Photo by Richard Aaron

Photo by Neil Zlozower

STANLEY CLARKE

Stanley Clarke, along with Jaco, is responsible for the bass being viewed as a legitimate solo instrument. To this end, he worked with Fodera basses to create the first six-string, allowing the bass to speak out in a true tenor range. Alongside fellow legend Chick Corea in the '70s fusion group Return to Forever, and subsequently as a solo artist, Clarke has taken the bass guitar into never-before imagined realms. Check out "School Days" and "Magician" to hear him in action.

JOHN PAUL JONES

As one of the founding members of rock icons Led Zeppelin, John Paul Jones inspired a world of bassists with his memorable, melodic lines. As one half of the dynamic rhythm section that also featured legendary drummer John Bonham, Jones filled out the bottom, in style, for countless Zeppelin classics. Check out "Ramble On" and "What Is and What Should Never Be" for quintessential Jones lines.

Photo by Robert Knight

Photo by Neil Zlozower

MARCUS MILLER

Marcus Miller is far more than just an outstanding bass player who grooves and solos with the best of them. He's also a top-notch producer and all-around musician who draws from many styles, including R&B, funk, hip hop, and jazz, to create a completely original sound that defies categorization. Aside from his notable work with Miles Davis in the early '80s, he's enjoyed a successful solo career in the midst of innumerable session appearances. Check out "Panther" and "Power" for examples of his formidable bass prowess.

JOHN ENTWISTLE

As the bass man for one of the biggest (and loudest!) rock bands of all time, the Who, John Entwistle has earned the names "The Ox" and "Thunderfingers." Possessing considerable chops and an explosive style, he was one of the first to inject bass solos, prominent fills, and counter melodies into pop songs. After bashing it out with Pete Townshend and Keith Moon at deafening volumes throughout the '60s, he went on to a solo career. Check out "Won't Get Fooled Again" and "The Real Me" for classic Entwistle performances.

Photo by Richard Aaron

Photo by Robert Knight

TONY LEVIN

From Peter Gabriel to Lou Reed to Paul Simon, Tony Levin has held down the bottom end for some of the biggest names in pop music. Besides being a founding member of prog-rock legends King Crimson (with whom he still tours), Levin has also widely popularized the use of the Chapman Stick, which he made use of on Gabriel's monumental *So* album. His list of session credits is staggering, as well. Listen to "Big Time" and "Heartbeat" for Levin at his finest.

FLEA

Red Hot Chili Peppers bassist Flea is a force to be reckoned with. Possessing a virtuosic slap-and-pop technique and a relentless source of energy, he's inspired a new breed of hardcore funk rockers. But he's far more than just a one-trick pony. He's graced some of the band's most sensitive ballads (e.g., "Soul to Squeeze") with beautifully memorable lines, as well. However, for classic Flea, listen to "Give it Away."

Photo by Jacques Brautbar/Retna

Photo by Michael Weintrob

VICTOR WOOTEN

Basically, Victor Wooten is a freak of nature. His virtuosity on the instrument is simply uncanny, not to mention unmistakable. He's taken the slap-and-pop technique into another dimension altogether, and it doesn't seem as though he's content to rest on his laurels either. As a resident member of the astounding Béla Fleck and the Flecktones, and as a solo artist, he's rewritten the rules of the instrument and continues to add chapters with each new recording. Just about anything from him is worthy of a listen.

APPENDIX

REFERENCE SHEET

Basic Bass Anatomy

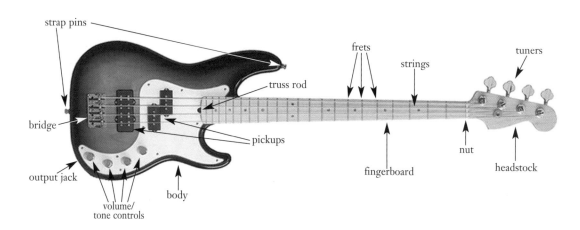

Notes on the Fretboard

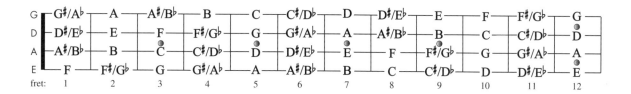

Triad Arpeggios

Major	Minor	Augmented	Diminished
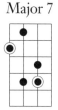	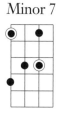	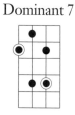	

7th Chord Arpeggios

Major 7	Minor 7	Dominant 7	Minor 7♭5
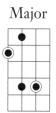	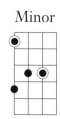	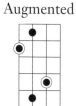	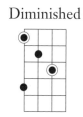

Modes

Ionian (Major Scale)

Dorian

Phrygian

Lydian

Mixolydian

Aeolian (Minor Scale)

Locrian

Additional Scales

Major Pentatonic

Minor Pentatonic

Blues Scale

Harmonic Minor

Melodic Minor

Chromatic

ESSENTIAL LISTENING

1. "Something," "Penny Lane," "Paperback Writer" (The Beatles)—Paul McCartney
2. *So* (Peter Gabriel), *Pieces of the Sun*—Tony Levin
3. *Highball With the Devil, Sailing the Seas of Cheese* (Primus)—Les Claypool
4. "Higher Ground," "Give it Away," "Soul to Squeeze" (Red Hot Chili Peppers)—Flea
5. "Addicted to That Rush" (Mr. Big), "NV43345" (Talas), "Shy Boy" (David Lee Roth)—Billy Sheehan
6. "Won't Get Fooled Again," "The Real Me," "My Generation" (The Who)—John Entwistle
7. "Ramble On" (Led Zeppelin)—John Paul Jones
8. "Good Vibrations" (The Beach Boys)—Carol Kaye
9. "Aquarius" (The Fifth Dimension)—Joe Osborn
10. *Disraeli Gears* (Cream)—Jack Bruce
11. *Nothing Like the Sun*—Sting
12. *Moving Pictures* (Rush)—Geddy Lee
13. *Ahh… The Name is Bootsy, Baby*—Bootsy Collins
14. "For Once in My Life" (Stevie Wonder), "What's Going On" (Marvin Gaye)—James Jamerson
15. *Jaco Pastorius*—Jaco
16. *M2*—Marcus Miller
17. "School Days," "Magician," "Lopsy Lu"—Stanley Clarke
18. *Yin-Yang*—Victor Wooten
19. "I Want to Take You Higher" (Sly and the Family Stone)—Larry Graham
20. *Funk on a Stick*—Paul Jackson
21. "In the Midnight Hour" (Wilson Pickett)—Donald "Duck" Dunn
22. "Cissy Strut" (The Meters)—George Porter, Jr.
23. "What Is Hip" (Tower of Power)—Francis Rocco Prestia
24. "Home at Last" (Steely Dan)—Chuck Rainey
25. *Bass and I*—Ron Carter
26. *Patitucci*—John Patitucci
27. *Mingus Ah Um*—Charles Mingus
28. *Ace of Bass*—Jeff Berlin
29. *Tribal Tech* (Tribal Tech)—Gary Willis
30. *The Book of Flame*—Michael Manring

WHO'S WHO MASTER LIST

Pop/Rock

1. Jack Bruce
2. Les Claypool
3. Tony Levin
4. Flea
5. Billy Sheehan
6. Stu Hamm
7. Doug Wimbish
8. Tina Weymouth
9. Sting
10. Geddy Lee
11. John Entwistle
12. Steve Harris
13. Chris Squire
14. John Paul Jones
15. Paul McCartney
16. Will Lee
17. Joe Osborn
18. Carol Kaye
19. Tommy Shannon

Funk and R&B

1. Bootsy Collins
2. James Jamerson
3. Marcus Miller
4. Victor Wooten
5. Rocco Prestia
6. Larry Graham
7. Anthony Jackson
8. Louis Johnson
9. Chuck Rainey
10. Donald "Duck" Dunn
11. Bob Babbitt
12. George Porter, Jr.
13. Paul Jackson
14. Jerry Jemmott
15. Mark King
16. Tommy Cogbill

Jazz/Fusion

1. Jaco Pastorius
2. Ron Carter
3. Marc Johnson
4. John Patitucci
5. Stanley Clarke
6. Charles Mingus
7. Jeff Berlin
8. Eddie Gomez
9. Ray Brown
10. Bunny Brunel
11. Dave Holland
12. Christian McBride
13. Gary Willis
14. Milt Hinton
15. Paul Chambers
16. Percy Jones
17. Michael Manring

TRACK LISTING

Here's a list of every audio example and where it appears on the CD. You can think of this as sort of an "audio index." (That sounds snazzier than "track listing," anyway.)

CD Track	Time	Description of Example	CD Track	Time	Description of Example
1		fingerstyle vs. pick	16	0:14	playing w/ the kick – ex. B
2		tuning notes	16	0:31	playing w/ the kick – ex. C
3		tuning with harmonics	17		playing around the kick – ex. A
4		rhythmic values	17	0:13	playing around the kick – ex. B
5		ties	17	0:29	playing around the kick – ex. C
5	0:11	dots	18		playing with the hi-hat – ex. A
6		fretboard diagrams to show position	18	0:13	playing with the hi-hat – ex. B
6	0:09	chord chart – ex. A	18	0:26	playing with the hi-hat – ex. C
6	0:22	chord chart – ex. B	19		playing opposite the hi-hat – ex. A
6	0:36	chord chart with rhythmic accents	19	0:17	playing opposite the hi-hat – ex. B
7		C major scale in whole notes	19	0:33	playing opposite the hi-hat – ex. C
7	0:24	C major scale in quarter notes	19	0:49	playing opposite the hi-hat – ex. D
7	0:34	G major scale in quarter notes	20		hammer-on
7	0:43	F major scale in quarter notes	20	0:09	hammer-on exercise – ex. A
8		more major scales	20	0:21	hammer-on exercise – ex. B
9		C minor scale	20	0:30	hammer-on exercise – ex. C
10		major and perfect intervals	21		pull-off
10	0:29	minor intervals	21	0:11	pull-off exercise – ex. A
10	0:45	augmented/diminished intervals	21	0:23	pull-off exercise – ex. B
11		root note approach – ex. A	21	0:33	pull-off exercise – ex. C
11	0:12	root note approach – ex. B	22		ornamental slide – ex. A
12		root notes with approach tones – ex. A	22	0:06	ornamental slide – ex. B
12	0:09	root notes with approach tones – ex. B	22	0:13	scoop slide – ex. A
13		root/5th approach – ex. A	22	0:20	scoop slide – ex. B
13	0:11	root/5th approach – ex. B	23		connecting slide – ex. A
13	0:21	root/5th w/ higher octave – ex. A	23	0:07	connecting slide – ex. B
13	0:38	root/5th w/ higher octave – ex. B	24		legato slide – ex. A
13	0:51	root/5th w/ syncopation – ex. A	24	0:10	legato slide – ex. B
13	1:02	root/5th w/ syncopation – ex. B	25		dead notes – ex. A
14		arpeggiation approach – ex. A	25	0:21	dead notes – ex. B
14	0:14	arpeggiation approach – ex. B	25	0:49	dead notes – ex. C
14	0:29	arpeggiation: 7th chords – ex. A	26		staccato
14	0:43	arpeggiation: 7th chords – ex. B	27		grace notes – ex. A
15		passing tones – ex. A	27	0:09	grace notes – ex. B
15	0:16	passing tones – ex. B	27	0:17	grace notes – ex. C
15	0:30	scalar runs – ex. A	27	0:24	grace notes – ex. D
15	0:43	scalar runs – ex. B	28		accent marks
15	0:59	octave transference – ex. A	29		repeat sign
15	1:13	octave transference – ex. B	29	0:14	repeat sign w/ specific directions
16		playing w/ the kick – ex. A			

ABOUT THE AUTHOR

Chad Johnson studied music at the University of North Texas from 1990–1995. In 1998, he became a senior music editor for iSong.com, an internet-based company that produced instructional guitar-based CDs. After leaving iSong.com in 2000, he began editing, proofing, and authoring books for Hal Leonard Corporation. He's written over 20 books for Hal Leonard, including *Pentatonic Scales for Guitar*, *Guitar Tapping*, numerous *Signature Licks* books, and the *Hal Leonard Acoustic Guitar Method*, among others. Currently, Chad resides in Milwaukee, Wisconsin, where he works for Hal Leonard as a publication editor, and keeps busy writing, editing, composing, and recording. For correspondence, write to: chadljohnson@hotmail.com.

HAL•LEONARD BASS PLAY•ALONG

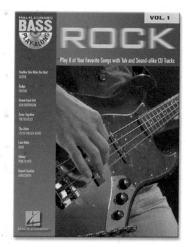

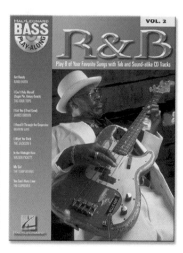

The Bass Play-Along Series will help you play your favorite songs quickly and easily! Just follow the tab, listen to the CD to hear how the bass should sound, and then play along using the separate backing tracks. The melody and lyrics are also included in the book in case you want to sing, or to simply help you follow along. The audio CD is playable on any CD player. For PC and Mac computer users, the CD is enhanced so you can adjust the recording to any tempo without changing pitch!

Rock VOLUME 1
Songs: Another One Bites the Dust • Badge • Brown Eyed Girl • Come Together • The Joker • Low Rider • Money • Sweet Emotion.
00699674 Book/CD Pack...$12.95

R&B VOLUME 2
Songs: Get Ready • I Can't Help Myself (Sugar Pie, Honey Bunch) • I Got You (I Feel Good) • I Heard It Through the Grapevine • I Want You Back • In the Midnight Hour • My Girl • You Can't Hurry Love.
00699675 Book/CD Pack...$12.95

Pop/Rock VOLUME 3
Songs: Crazy Little Thing Called Love • Crocodile Rock • Maneater • My Life • No Reply at All • Peg • Message in a Bottle • Suffragette City.
00699677 Book/CD Pack...$12.95

'90s Rock VOLUME 4
Songs: All I Wanna Do • Fly Away • Give It Away • Hard to Handle • Jeremy • Know Your Enemy • Spiderwebs • You Oughta Know.
00699679 Book/CD Pack...$12.95

Funk VOLUME 5
Songs: Brick House • Cissy Strut • Get Off • Get Up (I Feel Like Being) a Sex Machine • Higher Ground • Le Freak • Pick up the Pieces • Super Freak.
00699680 Book/CD Pack...$12.95

Classic Rock VOLUME 6
Songs: Free Ride • Funk #49 • Gimme Three Steps • Green-Eyed Lady • Radar Love • Werewolves of London • White Room • Won't Get Fooled Again.
00699678 Book/CD Pack...$12.95

Hard Rock VOLUME 7
Songs: Crazy Train • Detroit Rock City • Iron Man • Livin' on a Prayer • Living After Midnight • Peace Sells • Smoke on the Water • The Trooper.
00699676 Book/CD Pack...$12.95

Prices, contents and availability subject to change without notice.

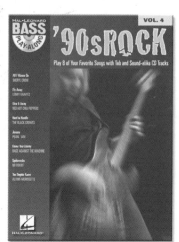

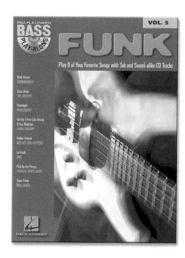

FOR MORE INFORMATION,
SEE YOUR LOCAL MUSIC DEALER,
OR WRITE TO:

HAL•LEONARD®
CORPORATION
7777 W. BLUEMOUND RD. P.O. BOX 13819
MILWAUKEE, WISCONSIN 53213
Visit Hal Leonard Online at **www.halleonard.com**